THE SOVIET INFANTRYMAN ON THE EASTERN FRONT

SIMON FORTY &
RICHARD CHARLTON-TAYLOR

CASEMATE | ILLUSTRATED

CIS0038

Print Edition: ISBN 978-1-63624-363-4
Digital Edition: ISBN 978-1-63624-364-1

Design by Eleanor Forty-Robbins
Printed and bound in the Czech Republic by FINIDR s.r.o.

CASEMATE PUBLISHERS (US)
Telephone (610) 853-9131
Fax (610) 853-9146
Email: casemate@casematepublishers.com
www.casematepublishers.com

CASEMATE PUBLISHERS (UK)
Telephone (0)1226 734350
Email: casemate-uk@casematepublishers.co.uk
www.casematepublishers.co.uk

Acknowledgements: The authors thank all those who have contributed, in particular Ruth Sheppard, Chris Cocks, and Lizzy Hammond at Casemate for constructive assistance in squeezing a quart into a pint pot, Eleanor Forty-Robbins (design) and Mark Franklin (artwork). The reenactment and equipment photographs are provided through the auspices of John Gibbon of the 13th Guards Rifle Division "Poltavaskaya." His history of that division formed the basis of the final section of the book on pp. 122–25. Thanks also to Marco Crolla and his models Jordan Lyle and Marek Oboril; Craig and Connor Palfrey (members of the 284th Rifle Division living history group) and Simon Vanlint (known as OTK87 online). Thanks also to Mikhail Moskalev for the repro smoking gear and to Olga Shirnina for permission to use her excellent colorized material. Please note that Olga makes no claim of copyright to the original versions of these photographs. We've tried to identify the provenance of these. If we've omitted anyone in error, please let us know through the publisher. Images credited to the Blavatnik Archive are used courtesy of Blavatnik Archive Foundation (http://www.blavatnikarchive.org/) Many of the quotations (identified by BA) also come from the Blavatnik Archive, which is dedicated to preserving and disseminating materials that contribute to the study of 20th-century Jewish and world history. The archive was founded in 2005 by the American industrialist and philanthropist Len Blavatnik to reflect his commitment to cultural heritage and expand his support for primary source-based scholarship and education. Thanks to Natalia Smotrov at the archive for her help. Finally, thanks to Piers for guiding us through the minefield of Russian spelling.

Page 1: "I was killed near Rzhev," a painting by Andrey Mironov, represents a line from an Alexander Tvardovsky poem which ends, "We fell for the motherland, But she is saved." Over eight million men and women of the Soviet armed forces died to defeat the invasion. Most of them were infantrymen—the *peshkom* (footslogger), *streltsi* (rifleman) or *frontovik* (front fighter). These soldiers were tenacious and tough, with a deep love of country. *Andrei Mironov/ WikiCommons (CC BY-SA 4.0)*

Pages 2–3: The position of the German advance on June 26, 1941. *Library of Congress (LoC)*

Right: An outstandingly brave female medic, Klarissa Cherniavskaia wears a *kubanka* on her head and the Order of Lenin on her breast. She served in a medical battalion of the Leningrad Front and was killed by a sniper on August 25, 1942. *Blavatnik Archive*

Contents

***Gimnastyorka* or *gymnastiorka*? Russian spellings**

There are always problems transliterating Cyrillic script. This is compounded—especially when it comes to place names—by changing international boundaries, historic usage (often German translations) and modern usage (e.g. Lviv, L'vov, Lwów, and Lemberg are all the same place). We have mainly used current Russian spellings (e.g. Pervomaysk and *telogreyka/ sharovary/gimnastyorka*) except for obvious anglicizations or usage (e.g .Kiev, Kharkov, Moscow, Stalingrad, etc.).

Timeline of Events

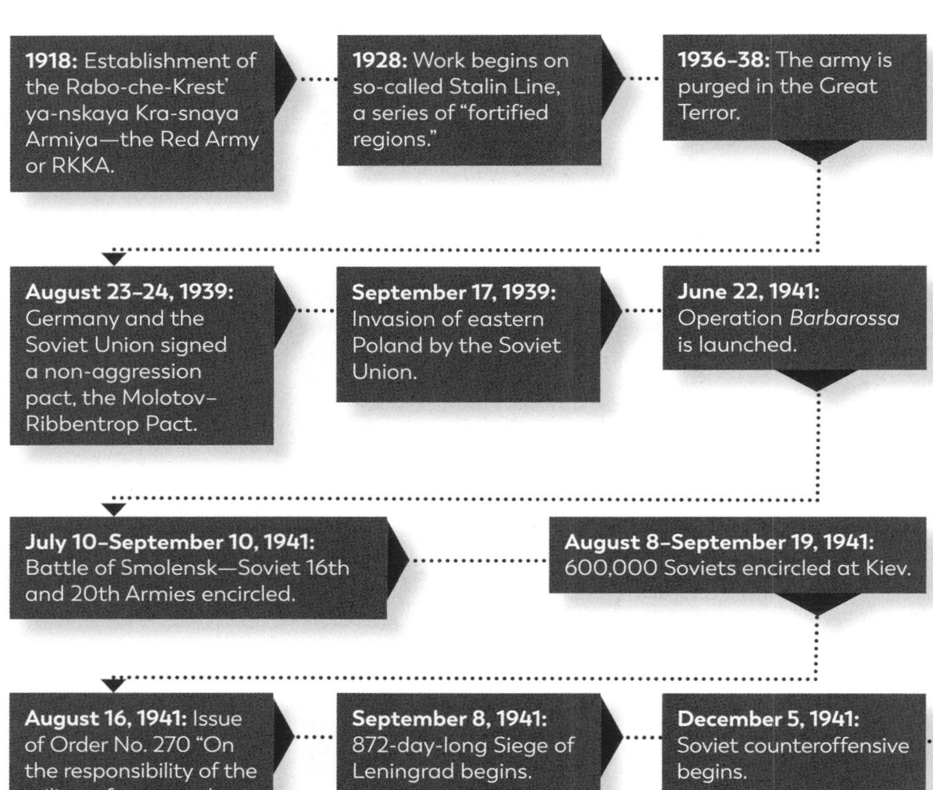

The Opposition. On July 19, 1940, following success in Poland and the west, Adolf Hitler promoted 12 generals to *Generalfeldmarschall*. Most of them would play a significant role in *Barbarossa*. L–R: Wilhelm Keitel, Gerd von Rundstedt, Fedor von Bock, Hermann Göring, Adolf Hitler, Walther von Brauchitsch, Wilhelm von Leeb, Wilhelm List, Günther von Kluge, Erwin von Witzleben, and lastly, Walter von Reichenau. *Narodowe Archiwum Cyfrowe/Polish National Archives (NAC)*

December 25, 1941: Soviet Kerch–Feodosia amphibious operation attempts to break the siege of Sevastopol.

May 12–30, 1942: Second battle of Kharkov; Soviets encircled and annihilated.

July 28, 1942: Issue of Order No. 227 "No Step Back!"

August 23, 1942: Battle of Stalingrad begins.

October 9, 1942: Abolition of military commissars in the Red Army.

November 19–23, 1942: Operation *Uranus* encircles German 6. Armee in Stalingrad.

November 25–December 20, 1942: Failure of Operation *Mars*, the Soviet offensive in the Rzhev salient.

February 2, 1943: Paulus surrenders 6. Armee at Stalingrad.

February 16, 1943: Kharkov falls to the Soviets in Operation *Zvezda* (Star).

February 21, 1943: Manstein's counterattack traps the overextended Red Army and retakes Kharkov.

July 5–16, 1943: Soviet victory at battle of Kursk.

Vyacheslav Molotov signs the Molotov–Ribbentrop Pact on August 23, 1939. Behind him, Joachim von Ribbentrop and Stalin look on. The pact's secret protocol led to the invasion and dismemberment of Poland by Germany and the Soviet Union. *NARA*

September–November 1943: Battle of the Dnieper. Germans successfully retreat across the river but Soviets establish bridgeheads.

January 4, 1944: Red Army crosses the border into Poland.

January 14–March 1, 1944: Leningrad–Novgorod offensive; Red Army advances to Estonia.

February 3, 1944: The Korosun pocket forms. Eight isolated German divisions are destroyed in two weeks.

February 21, 1944: Krivoi Rog on the Dnieper Bend falls.

March 26–April 14, 1944: The battle of the Crimea begins with the Odessa offensive; Sevastopol falls on May 9.

June 9–August 9, 1944: Soviets break through the Mannerheim Line; Gulf of Finland now open to Red Baltic Fleet.

Joseph Vissarionovich Stalin, General Secretary of the Communist Party of the Soviet Union, Chairman of the State Defense Committee and, from July 10, 1941, Supreme Commander of the Soviet armed forces. *NAC*

Stalin's Ten Blows

First mentioned in Stalin's speech on the 27th anniversary of the October Revolution, the "Ten Blows" started with the Dnieper–Carpathian offensive of December 24–April 17, 1944, and was followed chronologically by the Leningrad–Novgorod offensive, the Odessa offensive, the Vyborg–Petrozavodsk offensive, Operation *Bagration*, the Lvov–Sandomierz offensive, the Second Jassy–Kishinev offensive, the East Carpathian offensive, the Baltic offensive and, finally, the Petsamo–Kirkenes offensive that chased the retreating Germans out of Finland.

The idea of the Ten Blows implies a logic and strategic structure that almost certainly wasn't there. In fact, as Glantz has forcefully argued, the Soviet approach was to attack the Germans on a broad front and many of the successful operations were preceded by unsuccessful attacks that have been less well covered than the successes. What is indisputable is that 1944 saw the Red Army advance to the German borders, recovering its own territories and more.

June 22–August 19, 1944: Operation *Bagration* sees the Soviet advance to the Vistula.

August 19–October 14, 1944: The Second Jassy–Kishinev offensive forces Romania and Bulgaria to switch sides.

September 8–28, 1944: The East Carpathian offensive leads to the fall of Belgrade (November 24) and Budapest (February 13, 1945).

The Red Flag goes up in front of the parliament in Budapest. The Red Army swept through Romania, Bulgaria, and Hungary, reaching the gates of Vienna in April 1945. *Hungarian Archives (Fortepan/Vörös Hadsereg)*

September 14–November 24, 1944: The Baltic offensive sees Germans expelled from Estonia and Lithuania; Heeresgruppe Nord trapped in Courland.

September 19, 1944: Soviet Union signs Moscow Armistice with Finland.

January 12–February 2, 1945: The Vistula–Oder offensive ends with Zhukov 40 miles from Berlin.

February 4–11, 1945: The Yalta Conference planned the shape of postwar Europe.

March 16–April 15, 1945: Soviet offensive towards Vienna takes the city.

April 16–May 2, 1945: The Berlin offensive starts with battles along Oder and Neisse rivers. The last major obstacle before Berlin, the Seelow Heights, is taken on April 19.

May 7–9, 1945: German forces surrender to British, U.S. and Soviet forces.

Introduction

It is ironic that the capitalist countries of the Western world should owe such a debt to the Communist Red Army, doubly so because just over 20 years earlier the Allies—the United States, British Empire, French and others—supported the White Russians against the Reds. Never was the saying "the enemy of my enemy is my friend" more taken up than by both Western Allies and the Soviet Union in 1941 after the start of Operation *Barbarossa*. It may have been based on distrust, but the Lend-Lease program put in place by the United States and Great Britain was of substantial help to the Soviet Union—a country that had aided and abetted Germany to evade the military consequences of the Treaty of Versailles, had joined it in the dismemberment of Poland and had provided the Nazis with essential war materials.

Of course, supporting the Soviet Union helped the Western Allies: the sacrifice on the Eastern Front bled the Wehrmacht dry and left them ill-equipped to cope with the invasion of France when it happened. While the British and Americans played a massive part in the war against Germany—particularly at sea and in the air—there's no doubting where the major land battles took place as the table of German manpower on the Eastern Front shows. Between Operation *Barbarossa* and the invasion of Italy the bulk of German forces were in the east and thereafter the preponderance continued as they attempted to stem the Soviet advance—an advance that knocked Germany's allies out of the war, one by one. This is not to belittle the Western Allies' involvement which diverted not only men but, perhaps more importantly, the majority of the Luftwaffe's fighters to protect Germany from the strategic bombing campaign. The need to defend the Atlantic Wall also took much-needed raw materials—concrete and rebar for the bunkers; machine guns, mortars, antitank guns and artillery weapons for the defenses; and, of course, panzers for the mobile reserve. And then there

Eastern Front Manpower

	Axis total	*German (% in east)*	*Red Army Forces*
June 1941	3,767,000	3,117,000 (71%)	2,680,000 (in theater)
			5,500,000 (overall)
June 1942	3,720,000	2,690,000 (80%)	5,313,000
July 1943	3,933,000	3,483,000 (63%)	6,724,000
June 1944	3,370,000	2,520,000 (62%)	6,425,000
January 1945	2,330,000	2,230,000 (60%)	6,532,000
April 1945	c 2,500,000	1,960,000 (75%)	6,410,000
Total mobilised			34,476,700

Somewhere in the Persian corridor, a U.S. Army truck convoy carries Lend-Lease supplies for Russia in 1943. *LoC*

was the flow of Lend-Lease supplies to the Soviets: 12 percent of its armored vehicles, 15 percent of its combat aircraft, 25 percent of its foodstuffs, and around 50 percent of its trucks and jeeps.

The Soviet Union lost large tracts of land in the German offensive and this had a major effect on both available manpower and also on food production—from the start Red Army infantrymen complained of lack of food. Kumanev and Ryzhov quote First Deputy Chairman of the Soviet Council of Ministers, chairman of the State Planning Committee, Nikolay Voznesenskiy, from his book *The War Economy of the USSR during World War II*: "On the Soviet territory, under occupation, 7 million of 11.6 million horses that were in these areas before the occupation were exterminated or stolen by invaders; 17 million heads of cattle from the total number of 31 million were exterminated; 20 million pigs of the total 23.6 million; 27 million sheep and goats of the total number of 43 million." Crop production was reduced from 150,414,000 hectares in 1941 to 67,289,000 hectares in 1942. As the Germans closed on the Caucasus and Stalingrad, the Soviet Purchasing Commission in the United States requested more canned meat, fats, and oils, and by December 1942 food was given priority over other products. Most food came as concentrates and powders, necessary due to the length of the supply routes.

Also vital were metals—aluminum, cast iron, and various steels: over half of Soviet rails came from the United States, freeing Soviet industry to make tanks. Weapons were in short supply after the losses in 1941 and lack of metals increased manufacturing difficulties. While the importance of Lend-Lease shouldn't be over-emphasized—it accounted for only 5 percent of Soviet GDP between 1941 and 1945 and 80 percent of it was received after the battles of Stalingrad and Kursk when the Red Army was on top—the speed of Soviet success was helped significantly by the Allied contributions. It included 58 percent of the USSR's aviation fuel, 93 percent of its railway equipment, 50 percent of its TNT (1942–44), and 16 percent of its overall explosives.

Food supplied by Lend-Lease 1941–45

Product	*Supply vol in tons*	*Product*	*Supply vol in tons*
All food products:	3,983,000	Vegetable fat	465,000
Cereal products	1,044,000	Sugar	624,000
Meat products	787,000	Concentrates	330,000
Animal fat	625,000	Seeds	34,000

The Red Army had succumbed in summer 1941—as had the armies of Eastern Europe in 1940—to the might of the best-equipped, best-led, and best-motivated army of the time. Indeed, few forces in history were as capable as the Wehrmacht in that period. It had been honed by Blitzkrieg, its personnel and arsenal swelled by annexation and conquest. There were cracks: lack of strategic air forces, logistical issues, and the problems of the overlapping jurisdictions and power struggles of the Nazi elite, but these problems wouldn't become obvious until the opposition applied enough pressure to expose the failings—and it was in the east that this pressure was exerted.

It wasn't the Western Allies that stopped Hitler's all-conquering armies: it was the Soviet armed forces, and at the forefront the Red Army infantry. It was the Soviets—assisted by the terrain, the distances, and the weather—who cobbled together a defensive line and then provided the weight behind a winter counteroffensive that saved Moscow and Leningrad and stopped the Germans in their tracks. It was the Soviets who occupied 80 percent of the German Wehrmacht in 1942 and caused a German manpower and equipment crisis. It was the Soviets who ground out the victories at Stalingrad and Kursk that forced the Germans first onto the defensive and then into a retreat from which there would be no recovery.

The Red Army accomplished this while sustaining fearful losses as the table shows. It's also worth remembering that between 1941 and 1945, more than half the Soviet POWs (possibly as many as 3.3 of 5.7 million) taken by the Germans died in captivity. Additional to these massive casualty figures are the civilian deaths—as high as 20 million—not just from the fighting but from the executions and genocidal activities of the German extermination teams. The Soviets paid a heavy price for their victory, and it is unsurprising that their immediate postwar aims were to ensure Germany would not be able to fight again, and that a buffer of client states was put in place to protect their borders from any other western incursions.

The Theater of War

After 1922 the Bolshevik victors of the civil war took final control of the Russian Empire of the Tsars, which they transformed into the Union of Soviet Socialist Republics. Its huge area—8.6 million square miles spread over some 6,000 miles from west to east and 4,500 from north to south—represented about a sixth of the world's overall land mass. A quarter of this was European—up to the Ural Mountains—where most of the industry and population were. In 1940, there were about 194 million Soviet citizens divided among 11 Soviet Socialist Republics (Russia, Belorussia, Ukraine, Georgia, Armenia, Azerbaijan, Turkmenistan, Uzbekistan, Tajikistan, Kirghizstan, and Kazakhstan) and 19 major nationalities—each with its own language. After June 1940 also to be included were the Baltic states—Estonia, Latvia, and Lithuania (which also became Soviet socialist republics)—occupied by the Soviet Union as part of the Molotov-Ribbentrop Pact that had also secured the eastern half of Poland following the 1939 invasion.

Apart from the different nationalities and languages, the great geographical distances made control of the Soviet Union difficult, but there was a further significant division: religion. The Russian Empire had been staunchly Russian Orthodox. The Communist state promoted atheism—a problem for the Eastern Orthodox Christians and many Muslims whose places of worship were closed, and religious leaders persecuted. The other significant faith, Judaism, also saw its share of discrimination, although Lenin and the Soviet state were both against antisemitism. Indeed, large numbers of Jews fought for the Red Army and while many report strong elements of antisemitism, that tended to be a postwar issue and most Jews were accepted by their fellow soldiers without qualms.

The Russian winter is seen as one of the main factors in halting the German advance towards Moscow in 1941. This evocative watercolor was painted by Obergefreiter Fritz Brauner of Flakregiment 101, XXXXVII. Panzerkorps. Note the distinctive harness for the horse-drawn sled that proved to be the best transport system in the snow. The *panje* horses—related to the Polish *konik*, 12–13 hands high at the withers and weighing about 800lb—were used extensively by both sides. *RCT*

The terrain and weather of European Russia are both notable for their extremes, as identified by U.S. Army Pamphlet 20-290:

> Any attack from the west must hurdle [great] obstacles, and, at the same time, overcome the military resistance of the Soviets. In all that great expanse, only one major river, the Pripyat, flows from west to east and appears to provide access to the interior. But, of all the freaks of nature, just that river and its tributaries form such a maze of swamps that the watershed of the Pripyat constitutes an obstacle rather than a gateway to the interior of the USSR. Practically all other streams and rivers of the Soviet Union flow from north to south, though a few flow in the opposite direction. An attacker approaching from the west thus faces one natural obstacle after the other. As one proceeds toward the east, those obstacles become more and more formidable. The Dniestr, the Bug, the Neman, and the Dvina conform reasonably well to the usual concept of natural obstacles in the form of watercourses, although they are the very rivers that are peculiarly treacherous. The watersheds of the Dnepr, the Don, and the Volga constitute barriers of extreme difficulty. Moreover, the tributary streams of those watersheds combine with the main rivers to form what amounts to a perfect defense system. A look at the tributaries of the

Red Army Wartime Casualties

Period	*Total*	*Killed, missing, or captured*
1941	4,308,094	2,993,803
1942	7,080,801	2,993,536
1943	7,483,647	1,977,127
1944	6,503,204	1,412,335
1945	2,823,381	631,633
Official total	28,199,127	10,008,434
Likely actual total	35,000,000	14,700,000 (42%) of the total)

A mounted gun crew moving to a new position. Mud affected both sides: in autumn 1941 it delayed the German offensive at a crucial moment and allowed the Soviets to build up the Moscow defenses. In 1942, as the snows melted to mud, so the Soviet counteroffensive faltered. *RIA Novosti archive, image #90027/ Lander/WikiCommons (CC-BY-SA 3.0)*

> Dniestr on a 1:300,000 map, for example, shows that no military architect could have laid them out to any better advantage. ...
>
> Then there are the Russian forests, most of which merge with the swamplands. Northern European Russia is a woodland interspersed with swamps; the central part of European Russia abounds in forests; the southern part of European Russia is practically devoid of woods. As a matter of fact, European Russia is the only region of the Continent that has arid steppes and sand flats of typical desert character.
>
> Northern European Russia proper, that is to say the swampy woodland north and northeast of the Valdai Hills, is not suitable for mobile warfare, particularly not for large armored formations. The crucial blows of an offensive, therefore, have to fall in central and southern European Russia. In central European Russia lies the Smolensk–Moscow Ridge, a low glacial moraine whose western extension is known to the Germans as the Orsha Corridor (Landbrücke von Orscha). This is the watershed between the Black and Caspian Seas in the south, and the Baltic and White Seas in the north. Here are the sources of the Dnepr, the Dvina, the Lovat, and the Volga. Access to this ridge is of paramount importance for any conduct of military operations in the western part of European Russia. But the western approaches to the Orsha Corridor are protected by a wide belt of swamps and forests which extends from the Pripyat Marshes past Velikiye Luki and up to Leningrad. After breaking through this belt, an attacker still faces the watersheds of the Don and the Volga. Even if he has reached the Volga, an enemy coming from the west will find himself only in the outer ramparts of the Soviet domain; before him lie the Ural Mountains, and beyond them, Siberia.

As well as the rivers and associated swamps, the Soviet Union in 1941 was crossed by few metalled roads. Twice a year, just before winter and again in spring, rains and thaw bring on the *rasputitsa*, the bottomless mud that stops motor transport dead. At these times boats are better than cars or carts. The Germans hadn't done their research and, as Pamphlet 20-290 intimated:

> The field forces were taken completely by surprise by the first muddy season in the late fall of 1941 and encountered, in the fullest sense of the word, bottomless difficulties. Military operations that had been planned or had actually gotten under way became delayed or were foiled altogether. On the highway between Smolensk and Vyazma in late October 1941, for example, 6,000 supply trucks piled up, most of them loaded with ammunition, rations, and fuel for the forces advancing on Moscow. Not that the pile-up was caused by a failure to promptly replace demolished bridges with close-by

Fording rivers and lakes became second nature to the Red Army. Here sappers prepare a wooden bridge while an Su-85 takes a more direct route. *Colorized by Olga Shirnina*

emergency bridges; it was simply a case of the short approach roads to the emergency bridges disappearing time and again into the mud.

The German Army, dependent on horse-drawn transport, ground to a halt, giving time that helped the Soviets prepare their defenses around Moscow. In their turn, when it came for the Soviets to attack and push the Germans west, the rivers that had created such potential obstacles in 1942 proved easier to assault because of the reduction in German manpower and firepower. The Soviet infantry proved adept at fighting in forest and swamp and the Germans were less able to utilize the terrain in their defense.

Soviet Readiness

"Shock and awe"—if anything encapsulates the doctrine of the pre-emptive strike, the Nazi attack on its ally, the Soviet Union, on June 22, 1941, fulfills every requirement. Not only did it achieve almost complete surprise—despite intelligence reports made to Stalin—but its sheer power ensured that the Soviet response was kept off balance and proved futile. Generaloberst Franz Halder, OKH chief of staff, recorded in his diary:

> The enemy was surprised by the German attack. His forces were not in tactical disposition for defense. The troops in the border zone were widely scattered in their quarters. The frontier itself was for the most part weakly guarded. As a result of this tactical surprise, enemy resistance directly on the border was weak and disorganized, and we succeeded everywhere in seizing the bridges across the border rivers and in piercing the defense positions and field fortifications near the frontier.
>
> After the first shocks the enemy has turned to fight. There have been instances of tactical withdrawals and no doubt also disorderly retreats, but there are no indications of an attempted operational disengagement. Such a possibility can moreover be discounted. Some enemy HQs have been put out of action, e.g., in Bialystok, and some sectors are deprived of high echelon control. But quite apart from that, the impact of shock is such that the Russian High Command could not be expected in the first few days to form a clear enough picture of the situation to make so far-reaching a decision. On top of everything, the command organization is too ponderous to effect swift operational regrouping in reaction to our attack, and so the Russians will have to accept battle in the disposition in which they were deployed. Our Divs, on the entire offensive front have forced back the enemy on an average of 10 to 12km. This has opened the path for our Armor.

German troops pass border marker IV/95 on the right bank of the Solokiya River, Lviv Oblast, Ukraine. That area was attacked by Inf-Regt 57 of 9. Inf-Div, of Heeresgruppe Süd. It was guarded by the 2nd Border Outpost of the 91st Rava-Ruska Border Unit of the Ukrainian NKVD Border Guard. *Johannes Hähle WW2 Photo Archive/WikiCommons*

The German advances were staggering: by July 8 Halder could review the enemy situation:

> Of 164 identified rifle divisions, 89 have been totally or largely eliminated; 46 Russian combat divs. are on this front, 18 are tied down in other theaters (Finland 14, Caucasus 4), 11 are possibly still in reserve, in the rear. Of 29 identified armd. divs., 20 have been totally or largely eliminated; 9 still have full fighting-strength.
>
> The enemy is no longer in a position to organize a continuous front, not even behind strong terrain features. At the moment the apparent plan of the Red Army High Command is to check the German advance as far to the west as possible by draining our strength with incessant counter attacking with all available reserves. In pursuing this policy they evidently have grossly overestimated German losses. Meanwhile we must reckon with the attempt to activate new units, with which they might eventually stage an offensive. The plan of a large-scale disengagement is nowhere discernible.

The German victories skewed the manpower levels into the Germans' favor:

> Activation of new units, certainly on any larger scale, will fail for lack of officers, specialists and artillery materiel. This holds particularly for their armor, which even before the war was sadly lacking in officers, drivers and radio operators, as well as signal equipment. In the individual army groups, the situation works out as follows: North [*Nord*] which at the start of the campaign was numerically equal to the enemy, definitely outnumbers him after annihilation of numerous enemy divs. on its front; this superiority applies to both inf. and armor; Center [*Mitte*] which was stronger from the start now has a crushing superiority and can maintain it even if the enemy, as is expected, should bring new units to that front; South [*Süd*], which in the beginning was noticeably weaker in numbers, now has equal strength, due to the heavy losses inflicted on the enemy, and soon will add numerical to tactical and operational superiority.

Why was the Soviet Army blown away so easily? First, despite many intelligence reports predicting the invasion and even giving the date, the actual attack seems to have come as a surprise to Stalin. He and his government had done everything they could to not provoke Hitler, and to give themselves time to prepare for war, but didn't want to fully mobilize because that would constitute a threat in itself. There were definite reports of the impending hostilities from the border guards, from defectors, and from spies. These reports had led to the movement of troops west towards the frontier and also to additional call-up of reservists. The trouble was that when the German attack came, the speed of it gave little chance for full mobilization. By keeping their best troops near the border, the Soviets thought they would be able to buy time to fully mobilize. As it happened, all it meant was that they were chewed up more quickly than they would have been had they been held back. In particular, the

Russian Fixed Defenses, June 22, 1941

Location	*Length in km*	*Resistance centers*	*Bunkers built*	*Bunkers unbuilt*
1. Karelia	80	-	-	196
2. Kingisepp	70	-	-	89
3. Pskov	40	-	-	77
4. Polotsk	55	-	-	202
5. Minsk	160	-	-	206
6. Slutsk (started)	70	-	129	-
7. Mozyr	128	-	-	155
8. Korosten	185	-	-	455
9. Novgorod-Volynski	115	-	-	261
10. Kiev	85	-	-	217
11. Letychev	125	-	-	363
12. Mogilev-Yampil	140	-	-	276
13. Rybnitsa	120	-	-	236
14. Tiraspol	259	-	-	318
15. Ostrov	45	-	-	70
16. Sebezh	65	-	63	-
17. Shepetovka	110	-	137	-
18. Izyaslav	45	-	62	-
19. Starokonstantinov	60	-	-	158
20. Ostropol	50	-	89	-
21. Kamenets-Podolski	60	-	-	158
22. Sortavala	175	1	30	10
23. Keksgolm	80	4	-	-
24. Hanko				
25. Vyborg	150	1	130	44
Molotov Line:				
26. Telšiai	75	8	366	23
27. Šiauliai	90	6	403	27
28. Kaunas	105	10	599	31
29. Alytus	57	5	273	20
30. Grodno	80	9	606	98
31. Osowiec	60	8	594	59
32. Zambrow	70	10	550	53
33. Brest (-Litovsk)	120	10	380	128
34. Kovel	80	9	138	-
35. Vladimir-Volynski	60	7	141	97
36. Strumilov	45	5	180	84
37. Rava-Ruska	90	13	306	95
38. Przemyśl	120	7	186	99
39. Verkhne-Prut	75	10	7	-
40 Nizhne-Prut	77	17	8	-
41. Chernovtsy				
42. Danube	11			
43. Odessa	11			
44. Perekop				
45. Sevastopol				

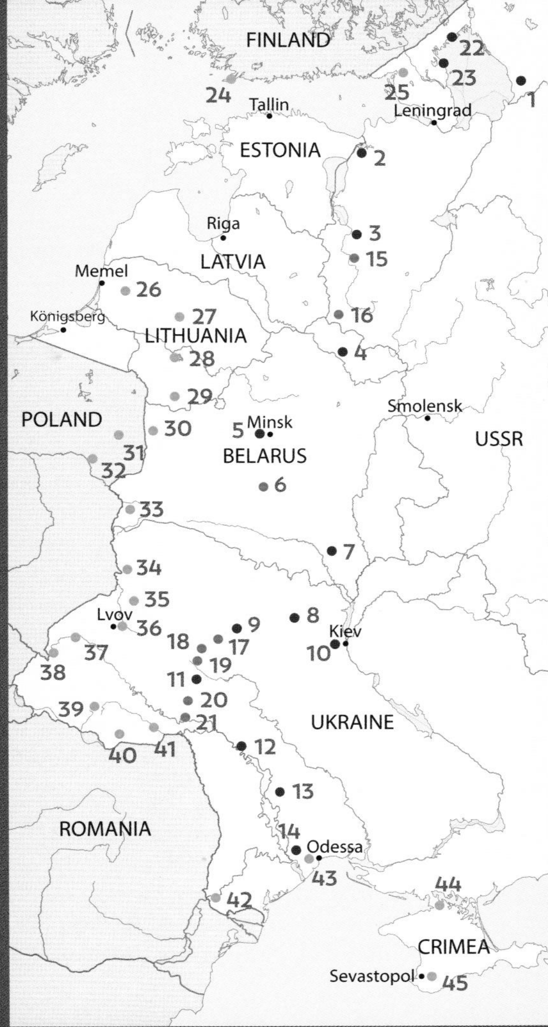

Dark Brown 1–14 = Regions constructed late 1920s–early 1938.

Red 15–21 = Stalin Line created in the late 1930s.

Orange 26–43 = Molotov Line started in 1940 on the new Russo-German border.

Not shown on the map is the fortified region at Murmansk.

Hanko was handed over by the Finns on March 22, 1940, after the Winter War.

The regions of Chernovtsy, Danube and Odessa were under reconnaissance.

The Crimean fortified regions were built up on earlier fortifications.

Info from Short (2008) and RKKA in World War II website.

Luftwaffe was able to destroy 800 Soviet aircraft on the first day. By end September the total was over 8,000 along with 200 of 340 military depots, over 20,000 tanks and around five million men. After the fall of Minsk on June 28, Foreign Minister Molotov reported that Stalin said, "Everything's lost. I give up. Lenin founded our state and we've fucked it up!" and disappeared into solitary confinement for two days. Whatever the truth of this, Stalin knew by then that the Red Army had been unable to mount an effective defense of Soviet borders, and that the defensive strategy had failed.

Part of the reason for this unpreparedness was the state of the fixed defenses that were supposed to withstand an assault. These had been started in the late 1920s at about the same time as France began construction of the Maginot Line. First built were the defenses at Polotsk, Minsk, Slutsk, and Mozyr. By the mid-1930s there were 13 fortified regions: Karelia opposite Finland; Kingisepp and Pskov opposite Estonia and Latvia; Polotsk opposite Lithuania; Minsk, Mozyr, Korosten, Novgorod-Volynskyi, Letychev, and Mogilev-Yampil opposite Poland; and Rybnitsa and Tiraspol opposite Romania. Kiev was also protected by a fortified region. Another tranche of building was undertaken in 1938–39 in eight more locations—the Ostrovsky, Sebezhsky, Izyaslavsky, Shepetovsky, Starokonstantinovsky, Ostropolsky, Kamenets-Podolsky, and Slutsky fortified regions. Stretching for nearly 2,000 kilometers, the line was never intended to be continuous, but the Stalin Line, as it became known, comprised a series of fortified areas with concrete pillboxes, barbed wire, minefields, and other fixed defenses.

Before the fortifications could be finished, the Soviet borders changed as Poland was divided up between the USSR and Germany, and the Baltic states were subsumed. The Stalin Line was abandoned and along the new frontier, the Molotov Line began construction. This line was also based on fortified areas. The big problem was that the Molotov Line defenses weren't finished, and the troops designated to defend the fortified areas were actually helping with the construction.

The Red Army had other problems. It didn't lack for men—indeed, it had undergone a significant expansion between 1939 and June 1941 as the boxed table shows. What it lacked was experienced men. One of the often-cited reasons for this was the Great Purge in 1936–38—the result of many years of doubt about the reliability of the army and Stalin's fears of the possibility of a coup. Apart from the obvious encouragement it gave to Germany, there's no doubt that the purges had an effect on the leadership—how could they not? In 1937, 10 percent of the Red Army's officers were dismissed. More went in 1938 at the same time as officer numbers expanded by over 50 percent. The real void was in the highest levels. While many of the dismissed officers would be readmitted to Red Army ranks in 1940, less replaceable were the corps, army, and military district commanders who had been purged and, in many cases, killed. Alan Bullock (1993) identifies 3 of 5 marshals, 13 of 15

Development of the Soviet Armed Forces

	Jan 1938	*June 1941*		*Jan 1938*	*June 1941*
Armies	1	27	Rifle brigades	0	5
Rifle corps	27	62	Mech (tank) corps	4	29
Rifle divisions	106	198	Tank divisions	0	61
Motorised divisions	0	31	Fortified regions	13	57
Cavalry corps	7	4	Airborne corps	0	5
Cavalry divisions	32	13	Airborne brigades	6	16

Total Strength 1,513,000 (1938) 5,373,000 (1941—a 255% increase)

army generals, 8 of 9 admirals, 50 of 57 army corps generals, 154 out of 186 division generals, all 16 army commissars, and 25 of 28 army corps commissars had been purged. Their places had been filled by officers with little senior experience. Junior officers were promoted too quickly, their training abbreviated. The Red Army lacked the professional NCOs of Western armies who held things together. The immediate result of the purges could be seen in the disastrous Winter War against Finland that started when the Soviets invaded on November 30, 1939. When the war finished three months later the Red Army had sustained around 350,000 casualties including around 150,000 dead and missing. The Finns suffered 70,000 casualties (26,000 dead). When *Barbarossa* started, over half the officers in the Red Army had been in position for less than two years. This inexperienced army—despite its size—couldn't withstand a huge attack by the well-oiled Nazi war machine.

On top of this, Soviet manufacturing couldn't keep pace first with the expansion of the army, and then with replacing losses. Metals were so scarce that water canteens had to be made from glass as they had in Tsarist days. The expansion of the army left critical weaponry and ammunition in short supply, and what there was, was often in the hands of untrained soldiers. These shortages got much worse after the huge losses caused by *Barbarossa*—Schechter dubs it the "demechanization" of the Red Army, and the personnel losses the "deprofessionalization." Shortages and lack of experience would dog the Red Army and lead to draconian orders to stem what the high command saw as a propensity to desert or retreat.

Ни шагу назад! (*Ni Shagu Nazad!*) No Step Back!

Much has been made of two orders—270 and 227—and how they affected the Soviet infantryman in particular. Schechter calls them "two key rulings on the use of violence as a motivator." They were certainly desperate measures taken at desperate times. Early in the war the NKVD was

No Step Back!

This mantra was promoted by propaganda and by two key orders. Order No. 270 on August 16, 1941, said deserting officers were to be shot on the spot and deserters' families were to be arrested. No. 277, of July 28, 1942, set up penal battalions (*shtrafbaty*) and companies (*shtrafroty*). Alexander Gak: "On occasion there were some people who fled. However, there were blocking forces positioned behind us and they would detain them. There were also instances of people shooting themselves to avoid going to the front. ... However, the medical commission was on the lookout for self-harm. People who shot themselves in the foot were executed by military tribunals to deter others from doing the same." (*BA*)

This photo shows what was reported to be an NKVD blocking unit setting up a Maxim machine gun. Alexander Gak witnessed an execution: "The regiment was lined up near a hill, so that stray bullets would hit the ground. The convicted men were lined up and the ruling of the military tribunal was read aloud: 'such and such are traitors to the Motherland and are to be executed for self-inflicted wounds.' An order to fire was given and the men were killed. However, it was all legal. This happened because the majority of people bravely and selflessly went into battle, never thinking about running away or inflicting harm to themselves." *SF collection*

ordered to detain deserters using blocking detachments. NKVD troops were formed into units to "lead a merciless fight against spies, traitors, saboteurs, deserters and all sorts of alarmists and disorganizers … Ruthless reprisals against alarmists, cowards, deserters who undermine power and discredit the honor of the Red Army are just as important as fighting espionage and sabotage." Soon, however, after the crushing early defeats the subject of desertion became a general order to be read out to the troops.

Blocking units had some effect. A report to Lavrentiy Beria, head of the NKVD (and organizer of the Katyn Forest massacre amongst other atrocities), on their effectiveness between June 22 and October 10, identified:

> From the beginning of the war through October 10 this year, special departments of the NKVD and barrage detachments of the NKVD troops for the protection of the rear detained 657,364 military personnel who lagged behind their units and fled from the front. … Of the detainees, the Special Divisions arrested 25,878 people, the remaining 632,486 people were formed into units and again sent to the front. … According to the decisions of the Special Divisions and the sentences of the Military Tribunals, 10,201 people were shot.

The trouble was that the order led to an excess of violence as officers were more likely to execute stragglers to ensure they themselves weren't killed—so much so that on October 4, 1941, Order No. 391 tried to curb these excesses. However, despite the order there was no getting away from the military realities and the retreats continued. *Fall Blau*, the German offensive that started in late June 1942, brought huge losses in the south as the Germans reached the Caucasus. Stalin reacted with order No. 227—Not one step back!

The effect was immediate. For example, the commander of the Stalingrad Front, Lieutenant-General V. N. Gordov, ordered on August 1:

> To the commanders of the 5th, 21st, 55th, 57th, 62nd, 63rd armies, within two days, form five barrage detachments, and the commanders of the 65th and 1st tank armies—

Order of the Supreme Command of the Red Army on August 16, 1941, No. 270

On the responsibility of the military for surrender and leaving weapons to the enemy

Not only our friends, but also our enemies are forced to acknowledge that, in our war of liberation from German-Fascist invaders, elements of the Red Army, the vast majority of them, their commanders and commissars conduct themselves with good behaviour, courageously, and sometimes—outright heroically. Even those parts of our army who, by circumstances are detached from the army and encircled, preserve the spirit of resistance and courage, not surrendering, trying to cause more damage to the enemy and to leave the encirclement. . . .

But we cannot hide that recently there have been some shameful acts of surrender. Certain generals have been a bad example to our troops. . . .

Can we put up with cowards in the Red Army, deserters who surrender themselves to the enemy as prisoners or their craven superiors, who at the first hitch on the front tear off their insignia and desert to the rear? No we cannot! . . .

Can we assume battalion commanders and commanders of regiments, who hide in crevices during combat, do not see the battlefield, and make no progress on the field of battle are regimental commanders and battalions? No we cannot!

I ORDER:

1. That commanders and political officers who tear off their insignia and desert to the rear or surrender to the enemy, be considered malicious deserters whose families are subject to arrest as a family, for violation of an oath and betrayal of their homeland.

2. All higher commanders and commissars are required to shoot on the spot any such deserters from among command personnel.

3. Encircled units and formations should fight to the last, to protect materiel like the apple of their eye, to break through from the rear of enemy troops, defeating the fascist dogs.

4. That every soldier is obliged, regardless of his or her position, to demand that their superiors, if part of their unit is surrounded, fight to the end, , and if a superior officer or a unit of the Red Army—instead of organizing resistance to the enemy—prefers to become a prisoner they should be destroyed by all means possible on land and air, and their families deprived of public benefits and assistance.

5. Division commanders and commissars are obliged to immediately shift from their posts commanders of battalions and regiments who hide in crevices during battle and those who fear directing a fight on the battlefield; to reduce their positions, as impostors, to be demoted to the ranks, and when necessary to shoot them on the spot, bringing to their place bold and courageous people, from among junior command personnel or those among the ranks of the Red Army who have excelled.

This order is to be read in all companies, squadrons, batteries, squadrons, teams and staffs.

> three barrage detachments of 200 people each. ... Barrier squads to subordinate the military councils of the armies through their special departments. At the head of the defensive squads put the most combat-trained special forces. ... Barrier squads should be staffed with the best fighters and commanders of the Far Eastern divisions. ... [They should] Provide road patrols.

The implementation was also immediate. The NKVD Blocking Unit reported on August 14:

> On the basis of Order No. 227, three army detachments were formed, each of 200 people. These units are fully armed with rifles, machine guns and light machine guns. ... Heads of the detachments appointed operational officers of special departments. ... The specified detachments up to 8.7.42 detained 363 people, of which: 93 people out of the environment, 146 lagged behind their units, 52 lost their units, 12 came from captivity, 54 fled from the battlefield, 2 with questionable injuries. ... As a result of a thorough check: 187 people were sent to their units, 43 to the staffing department, 73 to special NKVD camps, 27 to penal companies, 2 to a medical commission, 6 people were arrested and, as stated above, 24 people were shot before the formation.

By October 5, 1942, 193 army blocking detachments had been formed and they had detained 140,755 people since August 1. Of these, 3,980 people were arrested, 2,776 sent to penal companies, 185 to penal battalions, and 131,094 people were sent back to their units. 1,189 were shot. However, victory at Stalingrad and Kursk turned the tide and meant that the role of the blocking detachments altered. They took on several roles including protecting HQ echelons and lines of communication. On October 29, 1944, by order No 349, Stalin disbanded them.

Filtration Camps

"There are no Soviet prisoners of war, only traitors," Stalin is reported to have said. Certainly, anyone who was taken prisoner and escaped or was liberated, anyone who made their way back to Soviet lines after being encircled, or any stragglers picked up by the NKVD were sent to filtration camps. Boris Ginzburg was one of these, who having escaped capture eventually made it back to Soviet lines:

> I immediately found an officer and told him what had happened to me. I was immediately accepted back into the armed forces and assigned to the 86th Tank Battalion to be part of the tank-borne infantry. I was only there for a short while because Stalin issued an order to send all of those who had been in the occupied territories to special screening centers. These were special camps run by the NKVD.
>
> I think it was December 1942. I was sent to a special filtration camp along with others like me, as well as some scumbags. We were led away, far behind our lines. We were escorted by interior ministry troops ... [and] taken to Special NKVD Camp No. 178 in Ryazan where they began questioning us. I want to note that I was neither beaten nor insulted during the interrogations and that everyone I knew was treated more or less humanely. This is despite the fact that there were some real scumbags there including collaborators—policemen, *starostas*, and Vlasovites [after his capture, General Andrey Vlasov had denounced Bolshevism and defected to the German side]. ...
>
> One day, the camp commander summoned me. ... He notified me that the investigation into my case was finished, no compromising evidence was uncovered,

> and that they were sending me back to continue my military service. I was directed to the Ryazan recruitment office. Once I got there, I was questioned briefly about what my previous position was. Political deputy. I was made senior sergeant and sent to a unit. I found myself at the 1st Belorussian Front, where I began to fight. At first I was the assistant to the commander of a mortar platoon—my specialization was preserved. Later, when the platoon commander was wounded, I was appointed platoon commander. (*BA*)

Ginzburg's experience mirrors what happened to over 90 percent of soldiers in the filtration camps, about 8 percent of the remainder being arrested or condemned to serve in *shtrafbaty*. In 1945, about 100 filtration camps were set up for repatriated POWs and other displaced persons. More than four million people went through them. By 1946 the results were:

	Civilians	*POWs*
Freed	80%	20%
Redrafted	5%	43%
Sent to labor battalions	10%	22%
Transferred to the Gulag	2%	15%
Total	c 2.5 million	1,539,475

Encirclement

The brilliant German campaign of 1941 had led to a series of huge encirclement battles—*Kesselschlachten*—that netted massive quantities of prisoners and all but destroyed the Red Army. The lack of experienced NCOs and officers meant that the encircled forces stood little chance as Aron Chernyak outlined:

> All of a sudden, at the end of September and early October—October 2—the Germans launched an attack on Moscow, and we were utterly surprised when we found ourselves in the Vyazma encirclement. Not far from us the massive Bryansk encirclement formed.

Propaganda played a huge role in the Soviet Union—as it does today in Russia. This is the Memorial to the Panfilov Heroes, the 28 soldiers of General Panfilov's 316th Rifle Division who, on November 16, 1941, during the battle of Moscow, were said to have knocked out 18 tanks. All received the title Hero of the Soviet Union. Postwar research confirmed the story to have been a propaganda fabrication. *Valentina Martikhina/WikiCommons (CC-BY-SA 3.0)*

"Attack!" A 1942 postcard by artist V. Klimashin. *Blavatnik Archive*

> The size of this "pocket" that formed was about 120km in length, and 50–80km in width; the area was that size. The 16th, 19th, 20th, 24th, the 32nd Armies and a few other units found themselves encircled. One could say that the entire Western Front was encircled ... that there were no sizable units between us and Moscow. It was terrifying. ...
>
> Here's what encirclement entails. At the front, nothing was more terrifying. What's the worst thing about being encircled? Just imagine, we were young soldiers, young officers, and all of a sudden, all the lines of communication were severed. No delivery of supplies, neither food nor ammunition. Many commanders were at a loss of what to do; everyone's psychological state was horrible. Attempts were made to break out, and some did make it to the other side, but [successes] were few and rare. Within a week we came to the realization that we had no food or ammunition. We had nothing to shoot with, no shells. The worst of it was that we didn't know what to do. There was only one solution: ... We would try to get through in small groups of two, three, five people, [sometimes] seven. This was the surest way, if you can even say that. Hidden dangers were everywhere. For example, we faced serious danger when we had to cross the Minsk–Moscow highway. There was very heavy traffic: German tanks, artillery, cars ... even at night. It was frightening. ... I got out with one of my fellow soldiers, an Uyghur. ... He had a natural gift, an instinct that told him where it was safe to go. We emerged after about a month and half of wandering. We came out somewhere in Kursk Oblast, to the southeast. The military recruitment office questioned us, as did the NKVD. ... They asked us questions; this went on for no more than a day. Some people would get sent for further questioning for one reason or another. Anyway, we ended up in the assembly point of the military recruitment office and we were assigned to the 178th Reserve Rifle Regiment. (*BA*)

It's important to understand that the German assault was not as one-sided as perhaps it seems today, as one German field commander reported (in MS C-058):

> The so-called Stalin Line was held even more tenaciously, and the deeper we penetrated into Russia and the closer we came to Leningrad, the more we were amazed at the Soviet infantry's power of resistance, at its snipers, and its efficient defense tactics. The great battles of encirclement and the enormous numbers of PWs taken in the center of the Eastern Front later on do not alter my opinion; in those cases the Soviet commanders

1

4

2

3

Soviet Propaganda

1. "I will help you with Stakhanovite labor," a wife promises her husband as he leaves for the front in S. Adlivankin's 1941 postcard. This labor movement took its name from Alexei Stakhanov, a miner who produced 14 times his quota. Stakhanovites pushed themselves and others to work better and faster. The Home Front played an important role in the propaganda war.

2. *Novogodnii Baltiiskii privet!* Baltic New Year's greetings! The spire of St. Petersburg's Peter and Paul Cathedral and the dome of Saint Isaac's Cathedral are depicted in the background.

3. "For Motherland, for Stalin!" A 1944 postcard, part of the series "Glory to the Fighters of the Leningrad Front," shows the Red Army entering Germany.

4. This 1941 caricature depicts a red-eyed and sharp-toothed Hitler trying to escape the Red Army pincers. The paper reads "Program for the parade of the German troops on Red Square."
All Blavatnik Archive

"Don't let the Germans catch their breath!" This postcard catches the mood engendered by the winter counteroffensive of 1942. *Blavatnik Archive*

surrendered after they had been completely cut off from their lines of communication or because the situation in their respective front sectors had left them no other choice. …

We were soon forced to realize that we had underestimated our opponent; we had to adjust our tactics to those of the Soviet Army and had to learn a great deal. But by then the flower of our shock troops had been irretrievably lost, and today I feel justified in saying that this mistake, this ignorance of and underrating of the Soviet power of resistance, was one of the reasons for the failure of the German campaign against the U.S.S.R. … The Soviet infantrymen displayed outstanding skill in adapting themselves to the nature of the terrain and in utilizing it to the full, and they knew how to dig in within a surprisingly short time. Their system of positions was as simple as it was practical. They used trenches comparatively seldom; generally, two or three riflemen would occupy a deep and narrow foxhole. The machine-gun crews also occupied such foxholes, which were always well distributed and employed in such a manner as to leave no dead spaces. The best places were occupied by the snipers, of which each company had forty to fifty; frequently they were encountered perched on trees and in houses, always well camouflaged and hard to spot. If possible, the mortars were emplaced in natural hollows, or suitable holes were dug and reinforced; all calibers were available from the start of the campaign. …Thus, a system of defense positions in depth was established which was protected by wire entanglements and a large-scale use of mines. This method of defense was employed in any terrain—in villages, in level country, on hills, and in forests. …

Particularly impressive was the excellent combat discipline displayed by the Soviet companies. Usually, they allowed our patrols to penetrate their lines without harassing them, and even permitted them to withdraw without interference if they felt sure that the patrols had not learned anything. Generally, however, none of our men returned. As a rule, our reconnaissance planes saw little or nothing of the enemy, who remained motionless in well-camouflaged positions. I remember that German officers once drove in a motor vehicle through a seemingly deserted village. The officers were neither halted nor fired upon, and they saw no one. They swore later that neither soldier nor civilian had been in it. However, when we tried to occupy the village only a few hours later we found out that it was fortified, and when we finally captured it after fierce fighting, we found that it had been defended by an infantry regiment reinforced with weapons of every type. …

In the beginning of the Eastern campaign the Soviet attacks were not too impressive, and showed little initiative on the part of the Soviet command. They were carried out methodically, but cooperation with the heavy arms was inadequate and the lack of a flexible command was noticeable.

German Propaganda

Der Untermensch (The Subhuman) was a pamphlet produced under the auspices of Reichsführer-SS Heinrich Himmler in 1942. It lays out clearly what the Nazis wanted their soldiers to believe about the Soviet Union and its population: "[t]oday Bolshevism is the new Attila, the personification of the subhuman horde and its destructive power! But Bolshevism is not a phenomenon of just our time, not a product of our modern era. Neither has Bolshevism evolved within the framework of human history. Bolshevism is as old as the Jew itself! Lenin and Stalin are only two who have prepared the way for this new horde! ... Mulattos and Finn-Asian barbarians, gypsies and black skin savages all make up this modern underworld of subhumans that is always headed by the appearance of the eternal Jew. ... The German Aryan Knight stands as the bulwark against the subhuman horde, noble fighters for all that is good, keeping Europe from descending into the pit of savagery and stupidity. ... The subhuman will always be a subhuman, as a Jew remains a Jew, no matter by what name they call themselves: Churchill, Roosevelt, or Stalin. ... Either way we are repulsed by them and Stalin along with his allies and comrades is: Subhuman No. 1!"

Cover of the Nazi propaganda leaflet *Der Untermensch* (The Subhuman) produced by SS Main Office: "Bolshevism is the new Attila, the personification of the subhuman horde and its destructive power!" *www.holocaustresearchproject.org/holoprelude/deruntermensch.html/*

Much of the German propaganda linked anti-Semitism with anti-Bolshevism. This postcard features the poster for the anti-Semitic Nazi propaganda film *Der ewige Jude* (The Eternal Jew), featuring a caricatured Jewish man holding money, a whip, and a map of Germany with the Soviet hammer and sickle on it. The caption reads: "Major political showing in the northwest train station in Vienna on August 2, 1938. Open daily from 10:00 to 8:00." *Blavatnik Archive*

How Did the Soviets Turn It Round?

The Soviet defense stiffened at the end of 1942. Bravery, throwing millions of troops—often with insufficient training or weapons—into battle, assistance from the West, and the ability of the state to impose a total war footing that saw everyone heavily involved from the start: all these things contributed as did the phlegmatic character of the Soviet soldiers who were prepared to accept the many inherent privations. However, alone, these factors may not have been enough to turn the tide. Many of the territories the Germans conquered could have been turned against the Soviets—the recently annexed Baltic states had historically always fought against Russia. In general there were strong anti-communist feelings throughout the Soviet Union, particularly among those who had been affected by dekulakization—the redistribution of farmland that saw nearly two million peasant farmers deported in 1930–31—and collectivization, the move to state control of farms that had led to famines killing at least 10 million. As many as half of these deaths were in Ukraine, recently ravaged by the Holodomor famine that may have been part of the repression of Ukrainian independence or a result of the policies of industrialization and collectivization promoted by the Soviet state. Either way, the 1932–33 famine killed conservatively between three and a half and five million Ukrainians.

However, there was a big "but"—the genocidal views of Hitler and the Nazis that permeated every level of the German army, ensured that only a small percentage of the population under their control accepted their rule. This isn't to say that there weren't collaborators—some of whom were motivated by politics, such as the Vlasov's Russian Liberation Army, or those who joined the Ostlegionen—but many were coerced into collaborating, or chose to collaborate out of an instinct for self preservation by becoming *Hilfswillige* or Hiwis, "voluntary" auxiliaries. The number of Hiwis reached 600,000 by 1944. Many were captured Red Army soldiers who otherwise faced death as POWs.

Hitler, his generals, and many of his armed forces had a straightforward attitude towards the attack on the Soviet Union, as comments in Generaloberst Franz Halder's diary show. He identifies the German reasons for war as discussed in the Führer's office: the clash of the two ideologies.

Many Soviets were employed by the Wehrmacht. Some were coerced, while others chose collaboration rather than death or were POWs forced to work. Others—enemies of the regime, such as those who had suffered from dekulakization or famine, or were anti-Communists—volunteered and formed the Ostlegionen and Ostbataillone. Soviet troops were also used as police to protect establishments in the German rear areas and against partisans. Here, Russian policemen of Landesschützen-Bataillon 335, stationed in Smolensk, are photographed with a German officer and a soldier of the Wehrmacht. The policeman on the left is armed with a Steyr-Mannlicher M1890 carbine. *NAC*

> [Hitler gave] a crushing denunciation of Bolshevism, identified with a social criminality. Communism is an enormous danger for our future. We must forget the concept of comradeship between soldiers. A Communist is no comrade before nor after the battle. This is a war of extermination. If we do not grasp this, we shall still beat the enemy, but 30 years later we shall again have to fight the Communist foe. We do not wage war to preserve the enemy. …
>
> Extermination of the Bolshevist commissars and of the communist intelligentsia. The new states must be socialist, but without intellectual classes of their own. Creation of a new intellectual class must be prevented. A primitive socialist intelligentsia is all that is needed. We must fight against the poison of disintegration. This is no job for military courts. The individual troop commanders must know the issues at stake. They must be leaders in this fight. The troops must fight back with the methods with which they are attacked. Commissars and GPU men are criminal and must be dealt with as such. This need not mean that the troops should get out of hand. Rather, the commander must give orders which express the common feelings of his men.
>
> This war will be very different from the war in the West. Harshness today means lenience in the future. … Commanders must make the sacrifice of overcoming their personal scruples.

It is quite obvious what Hitler expected of his men: ruthless extermination. This was to be a war of annihilation with the exploitation of the resources—including slave labor—and, ultimately, the resettlement of the lands conquered by Germans. Civilians, POWs, and, of course, Jews were killed in their millions. The U.S. Holocaust Memorial Museum estimates that 17 million people were murdered by the Nazi regime and its collaborators between 1933 and 1945. Of these, over 10 million were Soviet, including at least 5.7 million non-Jewish civilians and 3 million POWs. The German Army was complicit in these murders from the start—right down to the infantrymen who either did the killing or handed prisoners to the SS-Einsatzgruppen behind the front lines.

These mass murders—unsurprisingly—did have a negative effect effect, convincing the Soviet population to support the Bolsheviks although many were distinctly unfavorable toward

The exterminations weren't limited to the Jews, commissars, and other groups the Germans found undesirable. This was a bitter war of annihilation that involved civilians, and the German military was complicit from the start—as this illustration shows. It depicts German soldiers ready to execute lined-up Russian peasants, as officers watch. Over 20 million Soviet civilians died during the war, through war, extermination, famine, and forced labor. *Blavatnik Archive*

the Communist regime. "What was Stalin unable to achieve in twenty years [that] Hitler achieved within one year? That we started to like Soviet rule," ran a joke in the Ukraine. Gerts Rogovoy expressed his feelings:

> I did not mention the hatred I felt toward the Germans. There is a town there called Kalach. Near Kalach we saw what had been a camp for Soviet POWs. The dead lay frozen in dugouts. Nearby stood stacks of railroad ties that they had placed there. Ties, corpses on top, then ties again ... some were burning, some were not. I had this urge, this sense of hatred toward the Germans ... In the sixties as a coin collector, I made contact with some Germans ... Only in the sixties did I begin to see them as people. Before that the very sound of the German language would make my insides churn, especially after I found out about Babiy Yar in which I lost my aunt and my cousin and the aunt's grandson. (*BA*)

The war in the east was brutal: "You want justice? You want fair play and decency? When you burn thousands of villages and bury children and old people alive in mass graves—then you don't think of justice, do you?"—a captured German officer was told by a partisan, after the former protested his rough handling.

Another result of the treatment of Soviet civilians by the Germans was the reciprocal treatment meted out by the Soviets as they advanced into German territory, raping and pillaging as they went. "Rage was a powerful incentive to kill—both on the field of battle and between engagements," Ilya Kobylyanskiy stated, explaining his hatred of the Germans. "As I fought on, I tried to take revenge on them for all of their monstrous offenses."

Having been under the cosh from the invasion and having suffered larger defeats than those that caused Western powers to surrender in 1940, the Soviet forces around Moscow were at the last moment helped by the extreme weather conditions at the end of 1941 and the arrival of reserves, many from the far east. With the enemy at the capital's gates, the Soviet counterattack halted the Germans in their tracks and allowed a regrouping. German logistical problems—partly a result of overconfidence and the arrogant belief that they would roll over the Soviet forces before the onset of winter—helped the defenders and dealt the German attack a mortal blow. The German successes in 1942 into the Caucasus masked their strategic failure in 1941, but the writing was on the wall. 1942 saw the Soviets grow stronger as the Germans followed Hitler's urgings to secure the oilfields in the Caucasus rather than push towards Moscow. The key battles on the Eastern Front took place at Stalingrad at the end of 1942 and then at Kursk in 1943 as Hitler's final Blitzkrieg campaign foundered against the minefields and prepared defenses of the Red Army. The Soviet infantryman played a crucial role in both battles and although losses were high, morale soared as the invaders were thrown back. Kurt Rogovoy was in Stalingrad:

> The time spent at Stalingrad was the most difficult in my life. ... There was a huge number of casualties: both ours and the Germans. Frozen. Despite the freeze, the smell was terrible. ... One time 45 of us were organized around three medium machine guns. ... I was in the vicinity of the Stalingrad Tractor Factory. There was a semi-destroyed building; we were told to take up positions there and not to retreat. The Germans were attempting to break out of encirclement in that area. We hung on for seven or ten days, I do not remember for sure.
>
> Only one of our three machine guns remained operational after that. The water coolers were damaged by mortar fire and the guns could no longer operate. We ran out

> of ammunition, then we ran out of food. The only thing we had left to do was die. When we ran out of ammunition for our last machine gun, we noticed an escape route. A shell had fallen nearby and blown an entrance into a basement. We climbed through the opening into the basement, and then another shell hit the same spot. We were covered in rubble. We were buried alive, and only had enough room to breathe. It was frightening: to be buried alive. How long was I there … maybe a day, maybe three, I am not certain. They say that a shell never hits the same place twice, but nevertheless, another shell hit the same place and made an opening. However, I was wounded; a piece of shrapnel hit me just under my left shoulder blade. (*BA*)

Defeated at Stalingrad, Hitler went back on the offensive at Kursk and launched his panzer divisions at the defenses the Red Army had prepared in depth. Mark Yankelevich was a gun layer for a 45mm antitank gun:

> We called [the guns] "Goodbye, Motherland"; they were placed in front of the infantry. I took part in battles on the Kursk–Orel Bulge, [operating] along dangerous tank paths … where for the first time the Germans began to use heavy Tiger tanks and Ferdinands. I was lucky. I knocked out a tank and was awarded the medal "For Courage." … We received instructions: only shoot at the mechanism that moves the caterpillar tracks. You needed to hit the mechanism that turned the caterpillar tracks. It so happened that at one point, four of us were still alive with two guns; we were carrying the shells ourselves. Armor-piercing shells did not work as the armor was very thick. … When I was in Kharkov, there were rumors of what was happening in Babi Yar. Anger made me act the way I acted. (*BA*)

Arkadiy Dayel was also on the 45mm guns. His graphic description of the action gives a taste of the dangers of being an antitank gunner in an infantry division:

> The tank approaching my trench was maybe 50 meters away, maybe less, coming toward me. I looked around and thought, well that's it, I am about to be crushed. One of my comrades was wounded in the arm; he was lying there all covered in blood. There were just two of us left. Who was manning the antitank gun? No one was there anymore, only the gun survived. I managed to grab it, and with two or three bullets we managed to take out that tank. Then we followed up with our machine gun. I received my first award for that battle, the Order of the Red Star. That was my most difficult battle.

The Red Army was able finally to defeat the Germans and take Berlin after heavy fighting in 1945. *Blavatnik Archive (Naum Secunda photo album)*

Soldiers marching in the snow. The infantry formed the core of the Red Army, as it did with every army of World War II, and suffered extremely high casualty figures. Unlike the Western allies, the Soviets didn't have critical personnel shortages, but they came close to it by the end of 1942 having suffered huge casualties and when over two million men of draftable age were in territory overrun by the enemy. *Blavatnik Archive*

> I and one of my fellow machine gunners survived. There had been three of us. One was hurt badly. He was lying right beside us. I don't even remember where or how he was wounded. He was taken away later. And there were two dead soldiers lying behind this long gun that I told you about, the antitank gun. My comrade and I, we grabbed this antitank gun together, and with two or three shots hit the tank. And later … It was hard to be fully aware of what we were doing, how … We tried to both shoot down the tank and stay alive. Then we fired the machine gun to finish them off. How many did we kill? No one fighting in the war could count who killed whom. Only a sniper could count that. They used to write: so-and-so killed two hundred Germans, another killed this many Germans … It's possible … I didn't keep track. (*BA*)

The Germans were held at Kursk and the story of the next two years was one of retreat for the Ostheer and increasing confidence for the Red Army in general and the Soviet infantryman in particular. They had gritty strength, as is identified in this view of the Russians as opponents provided by General Hellmuth Reinhardt postwar:

> a. The Russians apparently have an inexhaustible reservoir of manpower and that this manpower is employed with brutal ruthlessness. The Russians may accordingly be expected to employ large masses of men in their attack so in fighting the Russian numerical superiority will nearly always be encountered.
>
> b. The Russian infantryman, at least those recruited from the predominantly agricultural population, is much closer to nature than western soldiers. This explains their outstanding skill in finding cover, in camouflage, in creeping up to the enemy's lines and in infiltrating. Consequently, it is often difficult to combat them with long-range weapons, for they appear suddenly quite close by. The Soviet infantry has, moreover,

excellent marksmen, for their training is particularly stressed. Furthermore, the Russian infantry tenaciously hold on to any ground and never give up the terrain which they have once gained in an attack. As a result, hand-to-hand fighting is a special feature of operations against the Russians.

c. The Russians also are very skillful in the handling of technical means of combat. They may be expected to employ every available technical innovation. There is little reason to assume that they do not possess the same technical weapons and accessories as their potential enemy. It is remarkable how little the Russians allow themselves to be influenced by technical difficulties, and how, availing themselves of a sort of primitive technical knowledge, they quickly learn to bring their heavy weapons, tanks, and other mechanisms to bear in massed employment.

d. Russian soldiers are not insensitive to concentrated, heavy fire. This impresses them as much as the effect of rapid-fire machine guns. [The Russians termed the rapid-fire German Model 42 machine gun a "nerve saw."] This is also true of automatic weapons fired while on the move during the attacks of assault troops. The effect of this fire may lead to a temporary lowering in the Russians' aggressiveness and even to panic. The Russians very quickly regain hold of themselves, especially as the Soviet command habitually quells such manifestations with the severest countermeasures.

e. The Russians fight in every season and in every type of weather. Neither snow, ice, and cold nor rain and storm, nor fog or darkness prevent them from fighting. One can thus never count on a pause in the fighting due to weather conditions. Perhaps the only exception is that which occurs during the notorious "muddy period" though only then when it is at its worst.

f. The Soviet soldier, and particularly the infantryman, practically does not know such a thing as an "impassable" terrain exists. He can go everywhere, and he prefers terrain which, to the Western mind, presents insurmountable difficulties. Swamps, jungles, impassable mountains, and rivers are not obstacles to him.

g. One of the oldest Russian methods of waging war is to fight not only at the front but whenever possible also in the enemy's rear. The Russians are masters in this partisan-type fighting and have practiced and perfected it for over a hundred years. The characteristics noted above are widely present and aided by craftiness, cunning, and the imperturbability of the national character, and also by the nature of the Russian terrain.

RKKA Personnel Numbers

Date	*Field army*	*STAVKA reserve*	*Military district*	*Total*
December 1941	4,018,068	544,616	4,360,857	8,923,541
November 1942	6,605,498	202,965	3,800,620	10,609,083
January 1945	6,750,149	431,838	4,226,376	11,408,363

By 1943 the Soviet retreat had ended. After stopping the German advance at Kursk, the Red Army's progress west was continuous. Soviet historians see 1943 as the period of transition as the Red Army gained the strategic initiative from the Germans. 1944 saw them use the initiative to advance in great bounds that took the front lines to the borders of Germany itself. The confidence was palpable. Mikheil Milman remembers:

> By the time I got to the front, there was not a shadow of doubt left about the outcome, that we would win the war. Nobody could foresee how long it would last, it was only 1943, but nobody had a doubt that we would emerge victorious. I never saw anyone cross over to the enemy. I did see men who had self-inflicted wounds. They were afraid of combat and would rather stay in the hospital. (*BA*)

Operation *Bagration* was the beginning of the end for the Third Reich as it finally saw the Red Army retake the territories lost in the 1941 invasion. Mikhail Boguslavsky remembers:

> This was a difficult offensive that was meant to liberate Belarus. It was planned to be a fast-moving operation that did not involve long engagements with the enemy. The enemy was to be surrounded and bypassed. … On June 26 it began and by July 3 we had liberated Minsk. We bypassed Rogachov, without engaging the enemy, and other municipalities. It was incredibly difficult work. We marched day and night without any rest. We were fed on the go. We were given a piece of bread and salami which we ate without stopping. … Yes, we practically slept on the go. (*BA*)

The years 1944 and 1945 saw the Red Army sweep into the territories of the Nazis' erstwhile allies—Romania and Hungary—as well as advancing into the Baltic states and Poland. These territories would feel the Soviet occupation for many years to come, and their liberation was double-edged. One immediate consequence was the swelling of the Soviet manpower pool, as the armies of Romania joined Polish forces as part of the Red Army. The fighting continued into the streets of Berlin and, after Hitler's suicide, the Red Army pushed into eastern Germany, Austria, and Czechoslovakia to strengthen its position in the postwar world.

With casualties of almost three million, the first two quarters of 1945 took Soviet total losses from 1941 to nearly 30 million of which 8.5 million were "irrecoverable"—i.e., dead or no longer capable of fighting. This is a huge total, particularly when compared to to the losses of the Soviets' Axis opponents. While there are disputes about the actual figures which will never be completely resolved, the difference between the casualties of the two sides raises the question of why the discrepancy was so marked. Historians have debated the reasons for this, and several factors have been identified. First, the maltreatment of Soviet POWs saw many perish from malnutrition, overwork, or extermination. Second, the weakness of Soviet equipment when compared to that of the Germans, caused by the relative poverty of the Soviet state in the late 1930s as Davie cogently argues:

> The outcome of Poverty can be seen across the range of Red Army equipment, the tanks lacking good optical devices and electronics suffered heavy losses even when faced by standard German medium tanks such as the PzIV. Both sides in the war faced the need to increase the firepower of their infantry; [the] Red Army did this by going backwards to Great War technology, by issuing submachine guns which were powerful but short ranged and easy to manufacture. By contrast the German response was innovative, creating a new class of weapons—the assault rifle.

Third, the level of Soviet casualties produced a cycle that saw the dead and wounded replaced by poorly trained recruits thrust into combat to fill the gaping spaces. This left fewer experienced men in units to train the newcomers, even when units were pulled out of action to replenish their manpower. Red Army units were consistently under their intended strength.

Remarkably, the Red Army was able to defeat the well-trained and well-equipped German army despite its equipment issues, high level of casualties and lack of training. The Soviets did so not only through sheer numbers but because of the spirit of their fighting men. Like a boxer on the ropes, the Red Army stayed in the fight in 1941 and 1942 because it had to do so or face extermination. In the West, armies surrendered because they expected to be treated as outlined by international convention. By throwing away those conventions on the Eastern Front, the Nazi regime helped perpetuate the struggle that resulted in its own downfall. At the forefront of both losses and eventual victory was the Soviet infantryman.

Rewards

The Red Army understood the importance of encouraging morale by awarding medals and certificates of thanks. The recommendations for these decorations and awards were by commanders and military councils where relevant, and by the chiefs of arms and services. The main medals are shown in the table on pages 34–35. Yona Tsyganovsky remembers the joy and pride he felt when he received an award:

> During the war, I received four awards. My first was the Order of the Red Banner. I don't want to boast. It was the first order in our squadron. Here is how I earned it. We were near … Königsberg. The Germans counterattacked. Our troops had to retreat. Our battery commander was killed. We found ourselves semi-encircled. We held our ground for over 24 hours. We took down four German tanks. As the only surviving officer, I was in charge. Many were killed. Only five or six of us survived. ... I was summoned by the division commander. ... General Kushnarenko congratulated me. He gave me my award. Next, I saw the orderly. He handed me vodka and a sandwich. I got on my horse and headed back. It was autumn, I remember. It was cold. I unbuttoned my jacket. So everyone could see my award. I was so young, only twenty. You can understand. What an honor! Especially for a Jew to be the first?! (*BA*)

Not every example of bravery was recognized. Benjamin Poylin remembers Komsomol members being ordered to swim across the Dnieper. Only 34 made it, and they were not able to hold the bridgehead. In spite of their bravery and the casualties no awards were granted and the men were transferred.

Red Guardsman wearing from top left, the Order of the Red Star, Order of the Patriotic War (with ribbon), beneath is the Red Guards emblem, and next to that an RKKA Excellent Field Artilleryman. Unidentifiable medal on his left breast. His tunic is the *obr* 1943 woollen *gimnastyorka*. He shoulders a German MG 42. *Blavatnik Archive*

ЗА НАШУ СОВЕТСКУЮ РОДИНУ!

УДОСТОВЕРЕНИЕ.

ЗА УЧАСТИЕ В ГЕРОИЧЕСКОЙ ОБОРОНЕ

МОСКВЫ

Тов.

УКАЗОМ ПРЕЗИДИУМА ВЕРХОВНОГО СОВЕТА СССР от 1-го мая 1944 года НАГРАЖДЕН МЕДАЛЬЮ

„ЗА ОБОРОНУ МОСКВЫ"

ОТ ИМЕНИ ПРЕЗИДИУМА ВЕРХОВНОГО СОВЕТА СССР МЕДАЛЬ „ЗА ОБОРОНУ МОСКВЫ" ВРУЧЕНА 30 XII 1944 года

Record for the award "For the Defense of Moscow," October 1941 to January 1942. It was issued on December 30, 1944, to Leonid Isayevich Yakorevsky. During the defense of Moscow he commanded a platoon of a howitzer battery. Later in the war he was wounded twice and awarded Orders of the Red Star and Patriotic War, 1st Class, and the For Combat Merits medal. *Blavatnik Archive*

The Soviet Union issued its men numbered certificates of gratitude for advances and victories. No. 277, of February 13, 1945, was issued for the capture of the Hungarian capital: Budapest. No. 344, of April 26, 1945, was for the Czechoslovak city of Brno. This one, No. 359, was awarded to Max Grinberg after the defeat of the German defense of Berlin on the east of the city. No. 372, of August 23, 1945, was awarded for fighting the Japanese in the Far East. *Blavatnik Archive*

Приказом Верховного Главнокомандующего Маршала Советского Союза товарища Сталина от 1945 г. №

за

всему личному составу нашего соединения, в том числе и Вам, принимавшему участие в боях, ОБЪЯВЛЕНА БЛАГОДАРНОСТЬ.

КОМАНДИР ЧАСТИ

Soviet Medals

Top, L–R:

- Order of Glory. Awarded to lower ranks, usually for valor. Its three classes are comparable to the American DSC, Silver Star, and Bronze Star. Like the Gold Star, it carried with it a small pension. The highest rank to receive the Order of Glory is that of second lieutenant.
- Order of Suvorov. Awarded for distinguished services. Class I is for higher commanders; Class II is for corps, division, and brigade commanders and staffs; Class III goes down to certain battalion staff officers.
- Order of Bogdan Khmelnitsky. Awarded in three degrees. Each degree of this order ranks below the corresponding degrees of Kutuzov, which in turn rank below the corresponding degrees of Suvorov.
- Order of the War for the Fatherland. Awarded to both civilian and military personnel for arduous service in prosecution of the war.

Bottom, L–R:

- Order of Lenin. The highest civilian and military decoration of the USSR. Its award entitles the recipient to the title Hero of the Soviet Union.
- Order of the Red Banner. This order is the oldest of the USSR and dates from the Revolution. It is a unit award for outstanding service.
- 20 Years in the Red Army. Awarded for distinguished service since the first days of the Red Army. A very important and highly prized medal.
- Defense of Stalingrad. There are several Red Army Campaign medals awarded for service in famous defensive operations. Stalingrad is one.

U.S. War Dept Pamphlet No 21-30 "Our Red Army Ally" (April 1945)

Decoration	*Lowest rank of recipient*
Marshal's Star	Marshal
Hero of the Soviet Union, Orders of Lenin and the Golden Star (combined)	Private
Order of Victory	General
Order of Glory, Class I	ORs and air force junior lieutenants only
Order of Suvorov, Class I	Commander of arm or service at army level
Order of Suvorov, Class II	Chief of staff, brigade
Order of Kutuzov, Class I	Chief of staff, army
Order of Kutuzov, Class II	Chief of staff, brigade
Order of Bogdan Khmelnitsky, Class I	Commanders, brigade
Order of Bogdan Khmelnitsky, Class II	Chief of staff, brigade
Medal for 20 years in the Red Army	Private
Order of Suvorov, Class III	Commanders, company
Order of Kutuzov, Class III	Commanders, platoon
Order of Lenin	Private
Order of Bogdan Khmelnitsky, Class III	ORs and officers up to Commanders, battalion.
Order of the Red Banner	Private
Order of Glory, Class II	ORs and junior lieutenants only
Order of Alexander Nevsky	Commanders, platoon to regiment only
Order of the Fatherland War, Classes I and II	Private
Order of the Red Star	Private
Medal for Courage	Private
Medal for War Service	Private
Medal for Distinguished Service (by specialty)	ORs

The Soldier

The Nazis were able to instill their ideology in the German people during less than a decade in power: the Bolsheviks had had nearly two decades longer. The Russian Revolution and its aftermath had produced a generation of zealots, exemplified by the Komsomol, the Young Communist League, whose members were called upon to be in the forefront of industry and, after *Barbarossa*, on the front lines. In 1941 there were 11 million members, and many took their role seriously—as did Max Grinberg:

> Winter came. The snow came early, in October, in the north part of Sverdlovsk Oblast. A representative of the Komsomol district committee of the Novaya Lyalya District found out that there were Komsomol members … [where we were working,] so he came to see us. We happily volunteered to join the Red Army. Well, we were young, patriotic. We traveled to Novaya Lyalya and, after the formalities were taken care of, were sent to radio telegrapher courses in Sverdlovsk. In November 1941, at seventeen years old, I took the oath, and on that day my service began. We spent all winter on those courses. We trained for thirteen hours each day; half of it was devoted to Morse code. We spent so much time with the telegraph key that even now, after all these years, I still remember all the letters and digits and can still tap them out. We were trained thoroughly for two months. (*BA*)

The Soldier's Oath

I, a citizen of the Union of Soviet Socialist Republics, joining the ranks of the Workers' and Peasants' Red Army, do hereby take the oath of allegiance and do solemnly vow to be an honest, brave, disciplined and vigilant fighter, to guard strictly all military and State secrets, to obey implicitly all Army regulations and orders of my commanders, commissars and superiors.

I vow to study the duties of a soldier conscientiously, to safeguard Army and National property in every way possible and to be true to my People, my Soviet Motherland, and the Workers' and Peasants' Government to my last breath.

I am always prepared at the order of the Workers' and Peasants' Government to come to the defense of my Motherland—the Union of Soviet Socialist Republics—and, as a fighter of the Workers' and Peasants' Red Army, I vow to defend her courageously, skillfully, creditably and honorably, without sparing my blood and my very life to achieve complete victory over the enemy.

And if through evil intent I break this solemn oath, then let the stern punishment of the Soviet law, and the universal hatred and contempt of the working people, fall upon me.

J. STALIN, *Pravda*, February 25, 1939

The Soviet Union comprised many different ethnic groups, from Aleuts and Inuits in the east to Germans, Finns, and Poles in the west. Being able to speak Russian was mandatory. Even during the war, however, several ethnic groups were repressed—the Crimean Tartars, for example, were deported en masse to central Asia and were only allowed to return in the late 1980s. The ethnic composition of Red Army soldiers in 1941 was 61 percent Russian, 20 percent Ukrainian, and 4 percent Belorussian, with the remaining 15 percent being "*natsmens*," national minorities. By 1944, the army was 52 percent Russian, 34 percent Ukrainian, and 14 percent others. The officer corps had a similar composition but with an interestingly high proportion of Jews (about 5 percent). The higher the rank, however, the more likely it was that its holder would be Russian. *World War photos*

A Polyglot Army

The huge size of the Soviet Union ensured a multiplicity of ethnicitieswithin its armed forces. On June 22, 1941, the Red Army totaled some 5.4 million men. The first year of war saw losses of a similar level—casualties and men taken prisoner. Indeed, David Glantz itemizes the equivalent losses in the war's first 18 months as 297 divisions and 85 brigades. The level of casualties meant that while Stalin might have preferred to restrict who joined the army, the door had to be thrown open to older reservists, women, criminals, people in the Gulag, and non-Slavic ethnic minorities. This had the benefit of producing a totally integrated force—but it had drawbacks when it came to language. In 1942, the door was opened to citizens in liberated territories. On November 16, 1943, the Stavka authorized mobilization of 185,000 soldiers from them:

Front	*Number of men*	*Front*	*Number of men*
First Baltic	15,000	First Ukrainian	30,000
Western	30,000	Second Ukrainian	30,000
Belorussian	30,000	Third Ukrainian	20,000
		Fourth Ukrainian	30,000

While the bulk of the 34 million soldiers who served in the Red Army during the war were Russian, a third—some 13 million—weren't, including around five million Ukrainians, a million Belorussians, and the same number of Kazakhs and Uzbeks.

Komsomol membership badge. A youth organization of the Communist Party, Komsomol members were expected to show others the way. In a wartime diary, Leonid Ulitsky documented how: "I was elected the Komsomol organizer of my group ... around early April 1941, the Komsomol Committee called me into the office and asked, 'Do you know that clouds are gathering over our country?' Clouds as in war, clouds of war. I said, 'Yes, I read the newspapers.' 'The Komsomol Committee has discussed this issue and would like to ask you to talk to your group's Komsomol members and convince them to volunteer for the army.' I realized it was an order rather than a request ... I spoke to people and talked three more people into joining. We wrote to the military recruitment office volunteering to enlist into the army." *https://commons.wikimedia.org/w/index.php?curid=123627*

Another Komsomol member, Viktor Ginzburg, was determined to fight:

> It was 1942 and everyone's spirits were high because of our victory at Stalingrad. The secretary of the district Komsomol committee addressed the Komsomol members and said to us: "We are winning, but our Red Army needs help. We are inviting all first- and second-year students to volunteer for the Red Army." I should say that we earnestly wanted to fight. We thought that the war would be over any day and we would not get our chance to fight. What were we supposed to tell the girls later? That we sat far behind the front lines while the whole country was fighting … We were given applications and told how to fill them out. All the Komsomol members from the first and second years of university sat down and filled out their applications to join the Red Army. We were told that since we were students, we would all be sent to military academies. (*BA*)

It has to be said that as the war went on, sometimes this faith in their leaders slipped, as Benjamin Poylin relates:

> Finally, we reached Poland. There, [my beliefs were] shaken up for the first time. I knew that beyond [Soviet] borders, all the peasants lived in earth huts, dugouts. They have nothing. They are all poor. We crossed the borders and saw the actual houses of the peasant. Red brick houses! Houses with floors, not just dirt. They were living better than us! It was a shock, a real shock. I was the deputy political officer. It was difficult for me. Guys started asking me, "What's going on;" "Where's the bourgeoisie [we've heard so much about]?" And then we crossed into Germany. This had a serious effect. Serious effect on people's moral state. But everyone was afraid to speak up. SMERSH [Soviet spy detection agency] was working; everyone kept silent. (*BA*)

In 1932, Kliment E. Voroshilov—a Stalin loyalist, a member of the Politburo, and the People's Commissar for Military and Naval Affairs—put his name to the Osoaviakhim's Voroshilov Marksman's award. Two years later, the Young Voroshilov Marksman was set up. By 1936, over 20,000 Soviets had been awarded the first-class Voroshilov Marksman badge, and 1,000 the second class. In 1937, over 6,600 small-bore ranges were established in factories or workplaces across the Soviet Union for people to practice their marksmanship. *Osoaviakhim/WikiCommons*

Other organizations had provided quasi-military training: the Osoaviakhim being one such example. Open to any Soviet citizen, male or female, aged 14 or older, the Osoaviakhim—the Society for the Support of Defense, Aviation, and Chemical Engineering—was a paramilitary organization designed for military training. Of great importance was marksmanship and sniping—particularly after People's Commissar Kliment E. Voroshilov promoted it. "Learn to shoot like Voroshilov!" caught on, and in 1932 the Central Council of the Osoaviakhim approved the Voroshilov Marksman award, and two years later the Young Voroshilov Marksman. In 1937, over 6,600 small-bore ranges were established in factories or workplaces across the Soviet Union to allow practice shooting. During the war, the Osoaviakhim trained hundreds of thousands of antitank gunners, mortarmen and machine gunners.

On September 17, 1941, the State Defense Committee brought back the Vsevobuch—the Universal Military Training Administration, which had been created in 1918 and canceled in 1923—for males aged between 16 and 50. From then until 1945, nearly 10 million men were trained.

The Red Army Soldier

The Red Army acquired its infantrymen from several sources. First, and most obvious, were the volunteers and conscripts from the USSR itself. As the box on page 37 shows, that included many different peoples from a huge geographical area. Most of the conscripts were men, although large numbers of women also served—rather more on the front lines than is usually thought. The Red Army was policed politically by the NKVD, some of whose troops also found themselves fighting as infantry on the front line. Other Soviet troops included naval infantry and the armies of its allies that fought alongside the Red Army or as part of it.

The Red Army entered Bulgaria on September 8, 1944, and from the next day Bulgarian armies fought alongside the Soviets. Three Bulgarian armies totaling over 450,000 men fought in Yugoslavia, and then Hungary and Austria.

Starting off as an independent battalion, I Czech Army Corps fought with the Red Army from July 1942. It played an important part in the 1943 battle of Kiev, and subsequently at the Dukla Pass in 1944, and on into Prague in 1945.

The Ludowe Wojsko Polskie—the Polish People's Army—played an important role in the fighting all the way to Berlin (First Army) and Prague (Second Army). While many of the officers were Soviet, the LWP had a strength of over 200,000 at the end of the war.

Some 538,000 Romanian soldiers fought against the Axis after Romania changed sides in 1944. Of these, around 167,000 were killed, wounded, or went missing. Romanian forces fought in Transylvania, Hungary, Yugoslavia, and Austria.

Military service was obligatory in the Soviet Union from 1930, although originally limited to those over the age of 19. On September 1, 1939, the Law on Military Service was promulgated. This saw the period of service increased from two to three years and the age of conscription lowered to 17. It also abolished the right to conscientious objection. In October 1941, conscription was extended to all male citizens from the ages of 16 to 28. Soon, manpower issues required the conscription pool be enlarged so on February 9, 1942, conscription was widened to include citizens in liberated territories between 17 and 30. Love of the Motherland invaded by an aggressor, whose

"Onward! To the West!" Naval infantry units were formed by both the Red Army and Navy, and saw considerable action both as ordinary infantry and marines. The main theaters for naval operations were the Black Sea—where there were landings in Novorossiysk, the Kerch peninsula, and the Crimea—the Baltic, and major river crossings. *Kirill Belyayev*

ideology promoted a war of annihilation, meant that the Red Army wasn't short of volunteers to begin with, although high casualty rates meant problems soon arose.

Abram Kotlyar was born in Zhytomyr in 1924 and moved with his family to Kiev in 1935:

> I went to the army registry office and said—please, take me into the army. They didn't want to take me, I was still too young, I wasn't 17 yet. I was supposed to be 18 to get into the army. It took a lot of effort to persuade him … I became a cadet. Well, theoretically, military training in an academy should be a few years, but during the war, you graduated within six months. But because the Germans were gaining on us, our academy had to flee from the Germans. Our Academy was evacuated. We were retreating along the military cargo route, into the depth of the Caucasus, further away from Ordzhonikidze. It was horribly difficult to walk. Very hot. We carried all our things from the Academy with us, all our textbooks.
>
> We trained for only two months before we had to evacuate. Among us there were many Chechens, Ingushetians, Ossetians … many of them started running away, they didn't want to retreat any further. This was their home. Many of them were escaping into the mountains, deserting. … we got to some end point in the Caucasus and continued our training. We trained for two more months, although we had three months of training left, but because the Germans were gaining on us, our commanders decided to deploy us as a new unit formation, a separate tank fighter battalion, and sent us to the front. (*BA*)

Gerts Rogovoy helped to build fortifications near Kiev but was wounded in early July 1941. He was evacuated to the Donbas, where he worked on a collective farm before volunteering for the military.

> On July 10 the military recruitment office sent out draft notices to children born in 1925, 1924, and 1923, even though they were not yet of draft age. We were to report with our belongings, a spoon, and a mug. We were then led out of the city on foot. We crossed the Dnieper over the Chain Bridge. Then we traveled in cattle cars to the city of Stalino in the Donbas. We worked at the local collective farms. On the 29th Kiev was taken. I thought about how I had nowhere to return to. A few of us began visiting the local military recruitment office, requesting to be conscripted to the army. They refused categorically and cursed at us—the last thing they needed was greenhorn fools! But finally I was recruited as a volunteer before I had turned eighteen. Initially I served in reserve regiments, but

Enlisting for the front. Recruits entering Voroshilov Barracks in Moscow. Many have the M35 *veshchmeshok* duffel bag. They are fastened by string at the top, as duffel bags are; the long strap can be fastened across the chest making it a backpack. The loose end has a wooden toggle to fasten it back to the bag. *RIA Novosti archive, image #662758/Anatoliy Garanin/WikiCommons (CC-BY-SA 3.0)*

> when the Battle of Moscow began in November, I was deployed there and took part in combat.
>
> We were trained for a month in a reserve regiment. We had "state-of-the-art" rifles. The Russian Mosin 1901–1930 rifle. This wonder weapon was taller than me. I participated in the capture of several villages. I was awarded a "For Battle Merit" medal, which was rare at the time. During one battle we attacked a school building. A German threw a grenade out of the window of the destroyed school, and a piece of shrapnel got lodged in my buttocks … I was hospitalized. I spent about a month and a half in hospital, and then I was given leave. In August 1942 I was sent to a military school, in Balakovo on the Volga, near Saratov. The school had been transferred from Crimea; it was the Simferopol Mortar–Machine Gun School. … We were supposed to train for five months and graduate as junior lieutenants. However, we were not allowed to finish training. In November, all 450 of us were thrown into battle at Stalingrad. (*BA*)

There were, of course, draft dodgers and deserters. Roger Reese shows that the NKVD was able to round up a sizable number during the war: 2,846,000 of whom 251,408 were punished for draft infractions and 126,956 for desertion, a prosecution rate of 8.2 percent.

The conscript had to pass a medical examination—not always a given. Viktor Ginzburg went for his and "the medical commission found four of us unfit for the academy due to poor eyesight and we were sent to a temporary company." It turned out to be little different to other service, as he recounts:

> [The temporary company] was the 180th Independent Antiaircraft Battalion. [It] was sent to the front in March 1943. We were issued pea coats, felt boots, and warm pants. We were told that we would be taken to Leningrad in order to liberate the city, which was still under siege. That is why we were given warm clothes. Our battalion, along with our guns mounted onto flatbed cars, was taken north. All of a sudden, near Kirov, our train was turned around and sent south. We traveled around Moscow and found ourselves near Kursk on April 11. It was already spring, and we still had warm felt boots. We were ordered off the train and told to defend … The Germans were advancing on Kursk. We had to defend our strip of land against tanks, using antiaircraft guns. We took up positions on a hill near the railroad and began digging in. For three days we walked on the wet earth in felt boots before we were given new uniforms. We chopped down telegraph poles and made fires. We slept with our feet facing toward the fire. (*BA*)

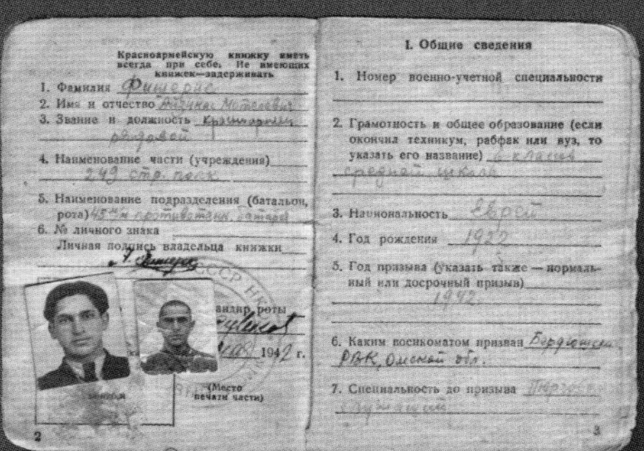

Красноармейскую книжку иметь всегда при себе. Не имеющих книжек—задерживать

1. Фамилия
2. Имя и отчество
3. Звание и должность
4. Наименование части (учреждения)
5. Наименование подразделения (батальон, рота)
6. № личного знака

Личная подпись владельца книжки

(Место печати части)

2

I. Общие сведения

1. Номер военно-учетной специальности
2. Грамотность и общее образование (если окончил техникум, рабфак или вуз, то указать его название)
3. Национальность
4. Год рождения
5. Год призыва (указать также — нормальный или досрочный призыв)
6. Каким военкоматом призван
7. Специальность до призыва

3

8. Место рождения и постоянного жительства. Домашний адрес, фамилия, имя и отчество жены или родителей
9. Группа крови по Янскому

Примечание. Общие сведения записываются в штабе части. Сведения о групповой принадлежности крови вносятся санитарной частью.

4

II. Прохождение службы

Часть, подразделение, занимаемая должность и звание	Месяц и число	Год и № приказа	Расписка командира роты

5

Red Army Record Book of 1942

These are the record books of Leonard Polyak (cover) and Aizik Fisheris (pages) from the Blavatnik Archive Foundation. This military identification and information booklet included current rank and position, biographical information, date of enlistment, current and past military units, and listed government-issued equipment and weapons.

PAGE 2

Always keep your Red Army book with you. Those not having books are liable to be detained.

1. Surname

2. First name and patronymic

3. Rank and position

4. Name of recruitment unit (establishment)

5. Name of unit (battalion, regiment) posted to

6. Personal ID number

Personal signature of book holder

Soldier's photo without headgear

Signature of CO and date

PAGE 3

I. General information

1. Military training specialism number

2. Literacy and general education (if technical college, worker's faculty, or higher education completed, provide its name)

3. Nationality

4. Year of birth

5. Year called up (also indicate Normal or Early call-up)

6. Called up by which Enlistment Office

7. Specialism before call-up

PAGE 4

8. Place of birth and permanent residence. Home address and full name of wife or parents

9. Blood group

Note: General information is recorded at unit HQ. Blood group information is given to the medical unit.

PAGE 5

II. Record of service

Unit, Subunit, Year and Regimental position and rank.

PAGE 6

III. Participation in campaigns, awards, and commendations

When and where—year and regiment that took part in battle.

For what awarded.

Notes to second and third parts

1. Notes are made by regimental commander by orders issued to the unit. On transfer to a different unit, record of service is signed by unit HQ head, with accompanying seal.

2. Notes on further service at the new place of service are made in the same section.

PAGES 7–10

IV. Clothing property

Item of/Quantity/Time

Clothing Issued/Returned

Winter hat (*ushanka* fur hat)

Cap (*pilotka*)

Forage cap

Greatcoat

Cloth (wool) tunic (*gimnastyorka*)

Cotton tunic

Cloth (wool) breeches (*sharovary*)

Cotton breeches

Waist belt

Trouser belt

Rifle sling

Strap for greatcoat roll

Backpack

Cavalry combat gear

Ammunition pouch

Hand grenade bag

Mess tin

Water canteen

Cover for mess tin

Cover for canteen

[Not shown, missing spread, pages 8–9, undershirts (summer and winter), underpants, towel, handkerchief, *portyanki* foot wraps (summer and winter), warm gloves, *sapogi* boots, ankle boots, puttees, half-length sheepskin coat, *valenki* felt boots, mattress cover, pillow, pillowcase, bed sheet, blanket.]

PAGE 11

Weapons and technical equipment covering Item of equipment/Quantity/Time Issued/Returned.

[The last three entries are all Degtyaryov light machine guns (7.62×39mm).]

PAGE 12 [not shown]

For soldier to note personal clothing sizes of: greatcoat, *ushanka*/*schlem* (fur hat), *furazhka* (peaked cap), *pilotka* (side cap), *sapogi* boots (jackboots), ankle boots, undershirt, *sharovary* (both summer and winter issue breeches), linen.

Between 1941 and 1945, such was the number of combatants permanently lost—killed, missing, captured, and sick—that the "army at the front had gone through 488 percent of its average monthly strength ... in other words it had been rebuilt five times." (Schechter, 2019) With that sort of turnover, it's unsurprising that the Red Army was made up of anybody the state could muster, no matter their gender or ethnicity. This is Efim Moiseyevich Stolyarsky, a Ukrainian Jew, who, having completed artillery school, was deployed in 1942 to the Northwestern Front with the rank of lieutenant. He took part in breaking through the Leningrad blockade, was seriously wounded near Riga, and was awarded two Orders of the Red Star, the Order of the Patriotic War, and two Medals for Battle Merit, as well as medals for the defense of Leningrad and the capture of Königsberg. *Blavatnik Archive*

This 1927 poster reads "Have you signed up for Osoaviakhim?" While it's hard to call the Soviet Union a militarized society in the same way that Germany was, there was nevertheless a great deal of emphasis on marksmanship and drill in societies such as the Osoaviakhim. *Kirill Belyayev*

Training

Once a soldier passed his medical test, he the soldier was sent for training—a process whose duration and efficiency depended on the state of the war. Complicated by language issues and shortages of weapons, the 1936 infantry manual was overhauled in late 1942 with lessons learnt in battle: "The 1st and 2nd parts … carry directives for tactical employment of men and infantry units (section, platoon, company, battalion), up to a Rifle Regiment inclusive, in conformity with the regulations regarding rifle units of the Red Army and experience acquired during the Great Patriotic War."

Benjamin Poylin was at university in Moscow when he was drafted. He trained in Siberia and tells of the advantages of this training:

> December 1941. I was in the 119th Rifle Brigade, left flank, defense of Moscow. We were on the side of Orel. I was introduced to the front lines there. I was lucky. I was trained in the Far East; training was fierce and strict. Freezing, cold, dirty, a snow forest. That's where we were taught how to fight. Our training was complete. When we got to Moscow, we felt strong. We quickly constructed shelters in the snow. We were in quilted pants, felt boots, hats. But we took our hats off, walked around in jerseys. We were fine. There was a group of Moscow volunteers; it was painful to look at them. They couldn't urinate because they couldn't open their zippers. Those poor guys. There was a mobilization of volunteers. Mobilization for death, literally. (*BA*)

On the other end of the spectrum was Arkadiy Dayel, who was raised in Volochys'k, Ukraine, but at the beginning of the war, he and his immediate family fled and ended up in Uzbekistan:

> I was drafted … into the army in 1943 … summoned to the city of Fergana. … [and] immediately drafted into a march regiment [a regiment containing replenishment troops], where they trained march companies for three or four months. Then I was sent to the front. … given the rank of *efreitor* [private first class] [and] appointed squad commander.
>
> It was very intense training. First, in terms of how we were dressed. This was Central Asia, where it's very hot. There was no rain during the period when I was in the army. We were starving. We received the so-called Soldier Ration No. 2. We were very hungry; it caused a lot of suffering. There wasn't enough food. The field where we practiced shooting was 7km from the city. We had to go on foot, of course. There was the famous soldier's

Lev Burshtein at artillery school in 1939. He had graduated from Kiev School No. 79—at the time specialized military schools were being opened in major Soviet cities with disciplines such as artillery, aviation, and naval. Burshtein continued his studies at the 12th Kiev Artillery Special School. Those who graduated summa cum laude—as he did—were sent to the 3rd Leningrad Semi-Academic Artillery School. He had completed two years of the three-year program when the war began. He was commissioned as a lieutenant, issued a uniform and military ID, and then dispatched to the Chief Directorate of Red Army Artillery Personnel in Moscow. *Blavatnik Archive*

> outfit devised by Marshal Timoshenko ... an overcoat, rolled up and worn over the shoulder, a rifle, gasmask, small digging spade, and a rucksack, which had to contain no less than 32kg of contents. ... 7km every day. Up at six, lights out at eleven. I witnessed two soldiers commit suicide. They couldn't handle these hardships. One soldier stood his rifle in a trench and threw himself on the bayonet, piercing his stomach.
>
> They taught us how to crawl flat on the ground, how to camouflage ourselves, how to hide; they taught us how to shoot. Then they formed the march companies. I was a squad commander, and I was trained to fire machine guns rather than rifles. I was assigned to command a Maxim machine-gun squad. ... It was very heavy, 70kg in total. You had to fill the barrel jacket with 4 liters of water and wait for it to boil. The ammunition belt was filled with 250 bullets, and the metal shield weighed 16kg. We had to carry all of this ourselves. (*BA*)

Women Soldiers

The number of women who served in the Red Army is difficult to appraise, but it's important to recognize that they were involved from the start. Many women tried to join up when the war began, with female Komsomol members particularly insistent. Most of them were channelled into "Home Front" duties, or work in industry or on the land. However, many were sent to military communications, as drivers and other rear area jobs. These mobilizations were often handled by the Central Committee of the Komsomol. One area in particular saw an immediate and significant influx of women: the medical services. As Pennington points out, "More than 40 percent of all Red Army doctors, surgeons, paramedics, and medical orderlies, and 100 percent of nurses, were women. Female medical orderlies and nurses served in the Red Army down to the company level." And these women were on the front line. There are many stories of bravery, such as those of women carrying the wounded from the battlefield under fire, retrieving them and their weapons. Pennington (2010) quotes Marshal Vasily Chuikov, commander of the 62nd Army at Stalingrad:

> [T]here was an orderly, Tamara Shmakova. I knew her personally ... Her evacuation method consisted of this: she would lie alongside the wounded man and, like an ant, dragged off her living cargo on her back, often one and a half times or twice her own weight. When it was impossible to lift a wounded man, Tamara spread out a groundsheet, rolled the wounded man onto it, and again on all fours, would drag behind her, like a tugboat, the groundsheet with the wounded man. Tamara Shmakova saved many lives.

After the losses of 1941, women were mobilized in spring 1942 (David Glantz identifies published documents that put the number between March 1942 and January 1943 at a minimum of 250,000 women). Many of these went to the Air Defense Forces (PVO). There were plenty of other non-combatant roles—from cooks to postal workers—that women filled. Others joined the air force—three all-female aviation regiments were formed by an order of December 1941. Women served as combat engineers, scouts, interrogators, and in tanks. As far as service in front-line infantry units is concerned, there's no doubt it happened. The Vsevobuch trained over 222,000 women including 6,000 on mortars and more than 15,000 on automatic weapons or submachine guns. It alone trained 4,500 women as HMG gunners and 7,800 on LMGs. Many took their places as commanders of companies and platoons. Pennington cites Zoya Smirnova-Medvedeva as an example of this, as she commanded machine-gun platoons and companies and ended up a junior lieutenant. The Voroshilov Infantry School in Ryazan had three women's battalions, and provided 1,400 women

A surprising success story, female snipers proved highly effective; the Central Women's School of Sniper Training was set up in 1943 to train them. Over 2,000 female snipers fought in the Red Army ranks. The most obviously successful was "Lady Death," Lyudmila Pavlichenko, although her official tally of 309 kills has been challenged by several historians. Pictured below, she's holding an SVT-40 with attached scope—in reality, she preferred the Mosin-Nagant. The Gold Star medal, which identifies her as a Hero of the Soviet Union, is on her chest. *Colorized by Olga Shirnina*

Soviet troops entering Bucharest. Note the proprietorial arm the soldier pictured top left places around the girl in the middle. While relationships were discouraged, many—condoned or not— still took place. Women in war who became romantically involved with soldiers were often derided as field wives (*polevye pokhodnye zheny* or *PPZhe*). As one medical assistant remarked: "There were only men around, so it's better to live with one than to be afraid of them all." ... "Women in the Red Army not only had to confront a lethally misogynist enemy but also at times a sexually predatory environment among their own male comrades-in-arms." (Sánchez Cózar, 2022) Senior army personnel—including Marshals G. K. Zhukov, I. S. Konev, and A. I. Eremenko—had "trophy" wives. Such was the widespread rumormongering about their relationships at the front that many women returned home seen as no better than prostitutes which, in turn, led to many women concealing what they had done in wartime, and not receiving the plaudits they had earned. *Online Photo Library of Romanian Communism Fotografia #C065*

platoon commanders in 1943; 704 took over rifle sections, 382 machine-gun sections, and 302 mortar crews.

Perhaps the most notorious service was as snipers. Prewar, women learned how to use weapons in shooting clubs and the Osoaviakhim. They proved to be excellent shots. Promoted by Komsomol, over 100,000 women went through sniper training courses during the war, and in 1943 the Central Women's School for Sniper Training was set up. Its 1,500 successful graduates are said to have been responsible for 11,280 enemy kills by 1945. The best-known woman sniper was "Lady Death"—Lyudmila Mikhailovna Pavlichenko; other. Other well-known women snipers were the team of Maria Polivanova and Natasha Kovshova, a duo who attained a total of more than 300 kills with the 130th Rifle Division of the 1st Shock Army before detonating hand grenades to kill themselves rather than be captured. Both were awarded the posthumous title Hero of the Soviet Union. Elsewhere, 50 women snipers commanded by Nina Lobkovskaya formed a platoon in the 3rd Shock Army, and were credited with 3,112 German kills.

As well as Pavlichenko, Polivanova, and Kovshova, 85 women became Heroes of the Soviet Union, 29 of whom were pilots and 26 of whom were partisans.

How many women served in total? It's difficult to say, particularly because of the condemnation of women soldiers as PPZh—*pokhodno-polevye zheny*, marching field wives. This unfair collective smearing of the many brave women who fought in the Red Army continued into the postwar period. Because of this, the reticence of the Soviet state to talk about their numbers and role, added to the lack of differentiation between the sexes often found in wartime documents, any estimate is likely to be incorrect. Officially, most Soviet works put the figure in the Red Army at 800,000 "at the front." The likely total number, including PVO and medical services, is well over two million with, Pennington suggests, around a million bearing arms—and many female medics and communications staff ended

Raisa Bruk with female colleagues. Three of them wear *ushankas*, the fourth (bottom left) a woolen head warmer. *Blavatnik Archive*

up fighting. Women also played a significant role in the partisan movement. Pennington assesses the figures in the following statement: "By 1944 there were a minimum of 280,000 active partisans; women filled 25 percent of the total, and 9.3 percent of operational roles, or approximately 26,000 active women partisans."

Penal Units

Order No. 227 ordered the formation of penal units to allow soldiers guilty of breaches of discipline because of "cowardice or bewilderment" to work off their guilt by being involved in hazardous missions. As they were put at dangerous sections of the front and commanded to redeem their sins by blood, many died. In all 427,910 *shtrafniki* served in the *shtrafbat* (battalions).

Date	*No. of* shtrafniki	*Date*	*No. of* shtrafniki
End 1942	24,993	1944	143,457
1943	177,694	1945	81,766

Between 1942 and 1945, 65 independent criminal battalions and 1,028 penal companies were established. The losses were substantial—in 1944, total killed and wounded from all criminal units amounted to 170,298—five times higher than the Red Army average. Those soldiers who ran afoul of their superiors were not the only ones who served as *shtrafniki*: other "criminals" were made to fight for the Red Army—around a million of them from the Gulags.

Usually, those sent to the penal units were there for a finite period—David Dushman said, "As a rule … you could get a ten-year sentence or three months in a penal unit, or an eight-year sentence of two months in a penal unit." After the period was up or you were wounded, there was a reasonable chance that you'd be returned to your unit—but this wasn't always the case. Anatoly Kibrik's unit fought next to a penal battalion: "They all dreamed of getting wounded, because after injury, as a rule, they were released and joined regular forces as normal servicemen, restored to their rank and military decorations." (*BA*)

The reasons for being sent to a penal unit were often quite arbitrary. Lev Ruderman was put in a penal unit

> because we did not carry out one of Stalin's orders. Everything that is done in the military is an order from Stalin. We were ordered to take a hill in Stalingrad—Staraya Otrada. … It was not very high. We took it five times, and every time the Germans knocked us out. Right away. Only nineteen people were left in our battalion. Only nineteen. The last time, the Germans drove us off to the third line. … That was it. We did not carry out

> Stalin's order. My battalion commander was a captain … He was wounded. We had a trial by court martial. He [was sentenced] to execution, I [was sent] to the penal unit. … People were sentenced to penal battalions and companies … But not for what you might think, like treason or something. (*BA*)

Semyon Rabovsky remembers that one "of our battalion commanders got lost and was sent to a penal company. He fought in that penal company, was wounded, and then came back to us." Mikhail Liderman was scared to death when he had his rifle and rain cape stolen:

> The rain cape didn't matter, but I couldn't show up in my unit without a rifle. There were some rifles standing there, so I took one and then snuck away … I went around the village searching and met a soldier from my unit. Usually telephone specialists were a sort of information bureau, because they had to lay the wires and knew what unit was where. So I found my battalion, my company. They were in a house, sitting outside in the garden, eating, and cleaning their weapons. They told me that if I had taken any longer to show up … they had started preparing the documents to declare me a deserter. And being declared a deserter means a tribunal and that'd be it for me … I could not have just joined any random unit. Nobody would feed you and you would be chased away. That is to say nothing of the SMERSH operatives that were embedded in each unit. It was the most terrifying organization. … There was one time someone in our company left his post for a short time, maybe to relieve himself or something. They shot him. This is terrible to think about. (*BA*)

Political Officers and the NKVD

As the Great Purge of 1936–38 showed, the state was always concerned about the political reliability of the army. One way that controls were exercised on the military leadership was using political officers and dual command. The political officers—the commissars—came under the control of PURKKA—*Politicheskoe upravlenie Raboche-krestyanskaya krasnaya armiya*, the Political Administration of the Red Army. PURKKA was initially under the command of Lev Mekhlis who had helped supervise the purge. Typical of his actions was the execution of the Kombrig (Brigade Commander) Alexei Vinogradov, CO of the 44th Rifle Division, his chief of staff Colonel Onufri I.

Israel Glushakov giving a political lecture in military unit, 1944. *Blavatnik Archive*

Stalingrad, September 23, 1943: a soldier, sailor, and political officer. It is impossible to separate the Red Army of World War II from the communist ideology of the Soviet Union. The dual command of units and separate rank system for political commissars were abolished on October 9, 1942, but political officers still played an important role in the army. Many were sent on military commander training courses, and 3,000 joined SMERSH. *Bundesarchiv 183-R0130-330*

Volkov, and the chief of the political department, Regimental Commissar I. T. Pakhomov, in front of the division following defeat by the Finns at the battle of Raate Road.

The position of political commissar dates to the years after the Revolution and the Civil War. Their role was reduced after the Bolshevik victory but was reinstated during the purges down to battalion level. They were responsible for political surveillance and were hated along with their informers. That many of them were Jews was a cause of antisemitism. The dual command allowed them to countermand unit commanders' orders—particularly if retreat was suggested. After all the failures and retreats, this role was officially abolished on October 9, 1942, with a decree that said that one-man control of the Red Army henceforth was the responsibility of the commanders, and that the positions of military commissar and political director were abolished. Politruks—deputy commanders for political affairs—would henceforth concentrate on morale-building and political work. In spring 1943, Efraim Paperniy was

> the [political officer] of the 9th and 10th Battalions [of the 1st Guards Fortified District]. What does it mean to be the political officer? It means you're on the front lines. It means you have to raise soldiers into action. It means you have to be in the middle. In the middle of the hell of war. How do you raise people into action? On the front line. Germans are attacking. There's fire exchange. The Germans advance. To execute a counterattack, you have to raise people into action. You have to scream and run ahead. Then the soldiers run after you. The soldiers follow you. (*BA*)

Abram Kotlyar explained the role of the political officers:

> He was a deputy battalion commander for political matters. He dealt exclusively with political things, like a [Communist] Party representative. He was an aide to the battalion commander. He had to motivate us, promote the party ideology. That's what a political officer did. (*BA*)

Hitler's Directives for the Treatment of Political Commissars

When fighting Bolshevism one cannot count on the enemy acting in accordance with the principles of humanity or International Law. In particular, it must be expected that the treatment of our prisoners by the political commissars of all types . . . will be cruel, inhuman and dictated by hate.

The troops must realize:

1.) That in this fight it is wrong to trust such elements with clemency and consideration in accordance with International Law. They are a menace to our own safety and to the rapid pacification of the conquered territories.

2.) That the originators of the Asiatic-barbaric methods of fighting are the political commissars. They must be dealt with promptly and with the utmost severity.

Therefore, if taken while fighting or offering resistance they must, on principle, be shot immediately. For the rest, the following instructions will apply:

I. Theater of Operations.

1) Political commissars who oppose our troops will be dealt with in accordance with the decree concerning jurisdiction in the *Barbarossa* area. This applies to commissars of any type and position, even if they are only suspected of resistance, sabotage or instigation thereto. Reference is made to "Directives on the behavior of troops in Russia."

2) Political commissars in their capacity of officials attached to the enemy troops are recognizable by their special insignia—red star with an inwoven golden hammer and sickle on the sleeves ... They are to be segregated at once, i.e., while still on the battlefield, from the prisoners of war. This is necessary in order to deprive them of any possibility of influencing the captured soldiers. Those commissars will not be recognized as soldiers; the protection granted to prisoners of war in accordance with International Law will not apply to them. After having been segregated they are to be dealt with.

3) Political commissars who are not guilty of any hostile act or are not suspected of such will remain unmolested for the time being. Only in the course of a deeper penetration into the country will it be possible to decide whether they are, or should be, handed over to the *Sonderkommandos*. The latter should preferably scrutinize these cases themselves.

4) As a matter of principle, when deliberating the question of "guilty or not guilty," the personal impression received of the commissar's outlook and attitude should be considered of greater importance than the facts of the case which may not be decisive. . . .

5) None of the abovementioned measures must delay the progress of operations. Combat troops should therefore refrain from systematic rounding-up and cleansing measures.

II. In the Rear Areas.

Commissars arrested in the rear area on account of doubtful behaviour are to be handed over to the *Einsatzgruppe* or the *Einsatzkommandos* of the SS Security Service respectively.

A sergeant and female soldiers of the SMERSH counterintelligence department of the 37th Army in Sofia, Bulgaria. Stalin ordered the creation of a counterintelligence service, SMERSH—*Smert' shpionam*, death to spies—in 1942. Its head, Viktor Abumakov, reported personally to Stalin. SMERSH not only searched for enemy spies but kept an eye on Red Army leaders, filtered soldiers returning from captivity, and was involved in controlling partisans. It was a wide remit that led to it being responsible for the torture and execution of many Soviet citizens and soldiers, as well as citizens from countries captured by the Red Army. *Central Archive of the Ministry of Defense Russian Federation https://tugulympu.ru/en/bolgariya-1944-45-let-totalitarnogo-rezhima-bolgariya-ne-prizna-t-chto/*

In reality, political officers were hated because of their association with the Special Section—a department of the NKVD that later became SMERSH—whose job was to listen out for treachery, but whose agents weren't above fabrication to enhance their positions.

The People's Commissariat for Internal Affairs (*Narodnyy komissariat vnutrennikh del*) was responsible for policing and, in particular, secret police activities. During the purges it was the NKVD that whisked people away in the middle of the night and either killed the unfortunates or conveyed them to the Gulag that the NKVD administered. In 1941 and 1942 the NKVD officers—the *osobists*—were judge, jury, and executioners. By October 10, 1941, they had picked up 10,201 deserters, of whom 3,321 had been shot in front of their units. These were the first of over 158,000 death sentences passed between 1941 and 1945. Semyon Rabovsky, when asked about deserters in his division, said:

> I remember only one single case. Maybe there were more, but in our regiment we had a case of self-inflicted injury. What does it mean? A young lieutenant shot through his hand to get to the hospital, but at the hospital they know how to differentiate self-inflicted wounds from assault injuries. They can determine by residue. He was sent to a military tribunal and sentenced to death by shooting. The officers were assembled, and he was shot in front of them.
>
> But in my unit we had no deserters. You see, we were on the offensive. Desertions occurred only during the German advance. In my battalion we had losses but no deserters. We retreated near Stalingrad, near Kharkov, but we didn't have them. Perhaps it happened elsewhere, but it was not common during an offensive for someone to desert. (*BA*)

As the Germans advanced, the NKVD executed over 100,000 political prisoners many because they couldn't evacuate them—particularly in Poland, Belorussia, and Ukraine. Katyn Forest is the site of such extrajudicial murders perhaps best known to Westerners. (The NKVD had already killed more than 111,000 Poles in the Great Purge of 1936–38.)

The NKVD raised 15 rifle divisions at the start of the war. By 1945 this had increased to 53 divisions and 28 brigades. They were mainly used as blocking troops and rear area security, although they also saw front-line action. The NKVD was responsible for handling the filtration camps that screened Soviet soldiers who made their way back to their lines after having been missing in action or taken POW.

"Partisans capturing a soldier in the woods"—a 1941 postcard illustrating the popular view of what was happening behind enemy lines in Soviet territories under German occupation. While there is much debate about their effectiveness—and at the time their relationship with the local population was soured by the way they took supplies, as well as German reprisals—there's no doubt that the partisan "menace" affected the Germans deeply, not only through what they did and the number of troops that had to be tied down either protecting assets or in anti-partisan operations but also psychologically. The partisan threat was also a contributory factor in a "shoot first, ask questions later" attitude that saw so many Soviet civilians murdered. *Blavatnik Archive*

Partisans

A large proportion of Soviet partisans were Red Army men who had been left behind enemy lines, either through escaping encirclement or simply by the speed of the German advance. Initially, most of the partisan activity was in those areas where the population was sympathetic (not in the Baltic states and less so in the Ukraine) and terrain was helpful—places where the forest and swamps helped hide movement and camps. More units coalesced in 1942, helped by troops—some of whom were parachuted in—and arms provided by the Red Army. In May 1942 the Central Staff of the Partisan Movement was set up and staffs attached to each front. These helped control and maintain the partisan units in the area. By December 1942 the number of partisans was up to 130,000, of whom around 40 percent were Red Army men. By January 1944 this had increased to 200,000 but during the year most were assimilated into the Red Army as it advanced and reconquered the lost territories.

On February 2, 1943, the "To a Partisan of the Patriotic War" medal was instituted. Here, a village priest is awarded a second-grade medal. *Fdutil/WikiCommons (CC BY-SA 3.0)*

Red Army Uniforms and Equipment

Soviet clothing and equipment proved reasonably durable and efficient during the war, with much materiel coming from Lend-Lease—although this wasn't always appreciated. Aizik Fisher:

> Our clothes were made in Britain. We had British overcoats. But we traded with the Russians, because Russian overcoats were better, warmer. The British ones were soft and light. And they traded gladly, especially the officers. We were better dressed than the Germans. The dead Germans [we saw] were practically half naked, without [proper] footwear. We had felt boots, wool socks. Our commanders had fur coats. But yes, we slept on the snow. (*BA*)

Following the Revolution, the Tsarist uniforms and ranks had been discarded, including the *pogony*, the shoulder boards. Rank and insignia began to return—they are necessary in even the most egalitarian of armies—and by 1940 there were patches for greatcoats, rectangular *pitlitsi* for collars, and officers' chevrons on the forearms. There was enameled or embroidered insignia depending on rank. The *pitlitsi* also carried branch of service insignia and colored piping, the latter also being found on headgear. In 1941 a subdued pattern of *pitlitsi* in green and without piping was brought out to be used in wartime. Metal was used in place of enamel and the service insignia were also usually removed.

Branch of Service Colors in 1940

Service	*Collar tab*	*Tab piping*	*Uniform piping*	*Cap band or piping*
Infantry	Raspberry	Black*	Raspberry	Raspberry
Cavalry	Blue	Black	Light blue	Black
Artillery/Armor	Black	Red	Red	Red
Technical troops	Black**	Blue	Black**	Black**
Chemical troops	Black**	Blue	Black**	Black**
Services	Dark green	Red	Red	Red

* Gold trim for officers. ** Raspberry for generals.

In 1943 the Red Army changed its uniform and insignia. As well as the uniform changes (see below), the most significant alteration was the return of the *pogony* that displayed rank and branch of service insignia as well as being piped in branch of service colors.

Wartime field headgear, L–R: officer's *furazhka*, officer's *pilotka*, *obr 40 ushanka*, private's *pilotka*, M41 *furazhka* with M41 subdued badge. *Craig and Connor Palfrey*

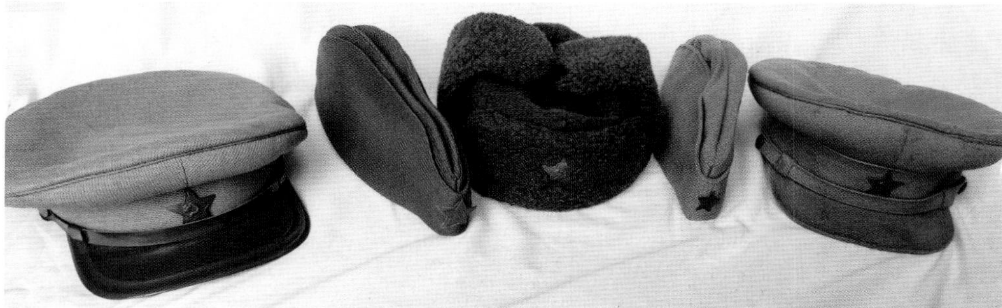

Prewar headgear, L–R: infantry officer's *budyenovka obr* 36, engineer private's *budyenovka obr* 36, private's *pilotka* (all branches), engineer officer's *pilotka*, engineer officer's *furazhka*. *Craig and Connor Palfrey*

Headgear

The development of Soviet helmets starts with the French M1915 "Adrian" helmet, on which the *Kaska* 1928 was based. This was superseded by the *Kaska* 1936, which can be seen in many wartime photos, and then the *Stal'noi shlem* (SSh) *obr* 39 and *obr* 40 steel helmets, the latter having six rivets that secured a new form of liner (three pouches of pads). Note: *obr* = *obrazets* = model.

Lighter-weight headgear was introduced on January 16, 1919, with the *shlem* or broadcloth helmet, nicknamed the *Bogatyrka* after the medieval *bogatyri* or, more usually, the *budyenovka* after Marshal Semyon Budyonny. A summer version was issued in white/khaki cotton. The *budyenovka* was replaced by the *pilotka* sidecap, which also came in cotton (summer) and wool (winter) versions. Officers' versions were of better quality and piped in branch of service colors. Stars were often worn—enameled red or subdued green—but often none in the field. Soldiers kept needles, thread, and a spare tunic collar liner in the folds of the *pilotka*.

Forage caps—*furazhka*—were worn mainly by officers and NCOs. The arm of service-colored piping and cap bands weren't used in wartime when an all-khaki field version was available.

There was also a M38 field hat for use in hot conditions. Troops called it the "*panamka*."

Helmets—right the SSh-40 helmet, standard Red Army helmet from 1940; below right, an SSh-36 standard prewar helmet. Note the small crest, which covered the helmet ventilation on the crown. Tests on Soviet helmets in 1942 showed that they were more effective than the Germans'. One reason for this was the weight, which made them uncomfortable to use for an extended length of time. Chronic lack of metals—and the fact that so many helmets were lost in 1941—meant that not everyone had this protection, as Isaak Rozenfeld remembered: "I got this [head] wound ... I did not have a helmet. ... They were not issued to us yet." But even when they were issued many people didn't use them, as Yona Tsyganovsky noted: "I was only wearing a hat on my head ... I was showing off by not wearing a helmet. Next to me there was a dead soldier in a helmet. At some point I decided to put on his helmet, and just a few minutes later there was an explosion, and I was nearly knocked unconscious. I was bleeding ... I still have a scar. A shell fragment pierced the helmet and was stuck right here." Brandon Schechter quotes a 1942 study from the Leningrad Front that found 83.7 percent of soldiers with head wounds were not wearing helmets. *Craig and Connor Palfrey*

Red Army Ranks After 1940

Marshal sovetskogo soyuza	Marshal of the Soviet Union
General armii	General
General-polkovnik	Colonel general
General-leytenant	Lieutenant general
General-mayor	Major general
Polkovnik	Colonel
Podpolkovnik	Lieutenant colonel
Mayor	Major
Kapitan	Captain
Starshiy leytenant	Senior lieutenant
Leytenant	Lieutenant
Mladshiy leytenant	Junior lieutenant
Starshina	Sergeant-major
Starshiy serzhant	Senior sergeant
Serzhant	Sergeant
Mladshiy serzhant	Lance sergeant
Yefreytor	Corporal
Krasnoarmeyets	Red Army man/Private

Note: The ranks of *Kombrig*, *Komdiv*, *Komkor*, and *Komandarm*, used from 1935, were changed when regular general ranks were reintroduced in 1940.

Top left: Sergeant-major Mikhail Vaysman in 1941–42. His *pitlitsi* would have been maroon with black piping (see opposite). In 1942 Vaysman completed a course for junior political officers and was assigned to a combat engineers' battalion in the 8th Guards Army. *Blavatnik Archive*

Center left: Senior Lieutenant Vaysman, 1945—note *pogony* (see also opposite). He was in Berlin on Victory Day. He received the Order of the Red Star and the battle Order of the Patriotic War, 1st and 2nd Class (the rays are golden in I class and silver in II class). Note also Guards insignia below medals and on his left breast pocket the Victory over Germany medal. *Blavatnik Archive*

Left: Leningrad, 1941. Soldiers march to the front. Note the two triangles indicating sergeant on the greatcoat collar gorget patches. *Vasily Fedoseev/ww2db.com*

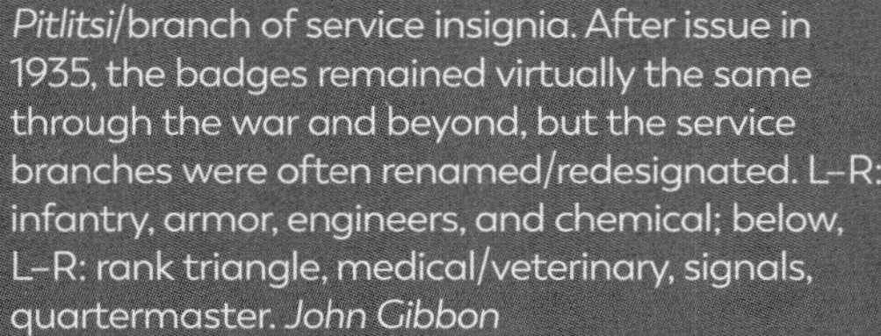

Pitlitsi/branch of service insignia. After issue in 1935, the badges remained virtually the same through the war and beyond, but the service branches were often renamed/redesignated. L–R: infantry, armor, engineers, and chemical; below, L–R: rank triangle, medical/veterinary, signals, quartermaster. *John Gibbon*

Infantry *pitlitsi* in maroon and black. Note the three triangles identifying the wearer as a senior sergeant and the infantry insignia. In wartime subdued versions were used (see below). *John Gibbon*

Below left: Subdued *pitlitsi* and greatcoat gorget patches showing rank insignia. Worn on uniform and greatcoat collars in 1941, these combined arm insignia and rank. The muted colors were used in action. *EF*

Below right: From 1943, the Red Army and VVS (Red Air Force) showed rank and arm insignia on shoulder boards (*pogony*). The piping identified the arm: maroon for infantry, red for artillery or armored troops, green for medical/veterinary, black for engineers, dark blue for cavalry, and light blue for VVS. *EF*

A *Krasnoarmeyets* (Red Army man), B *Yefreytor* (corporal), C *Mladshiy serzhant* (junior sergeant), D *Serzhant* (sergeant), E *Starshiy serzhant* (senior sergeant), F *Starshina* (sergeant-major), G *Mladshiy leytenant* (junior lieutenant), H *Leytenant* (lieutenant), I *Starshiy seytenant* (senior lieutenant), J *Kapitan* (captain), K *Mayor* (major), L *Podpolkovnik* (lieutenant colonel), M *Polkovnik* (colonel).

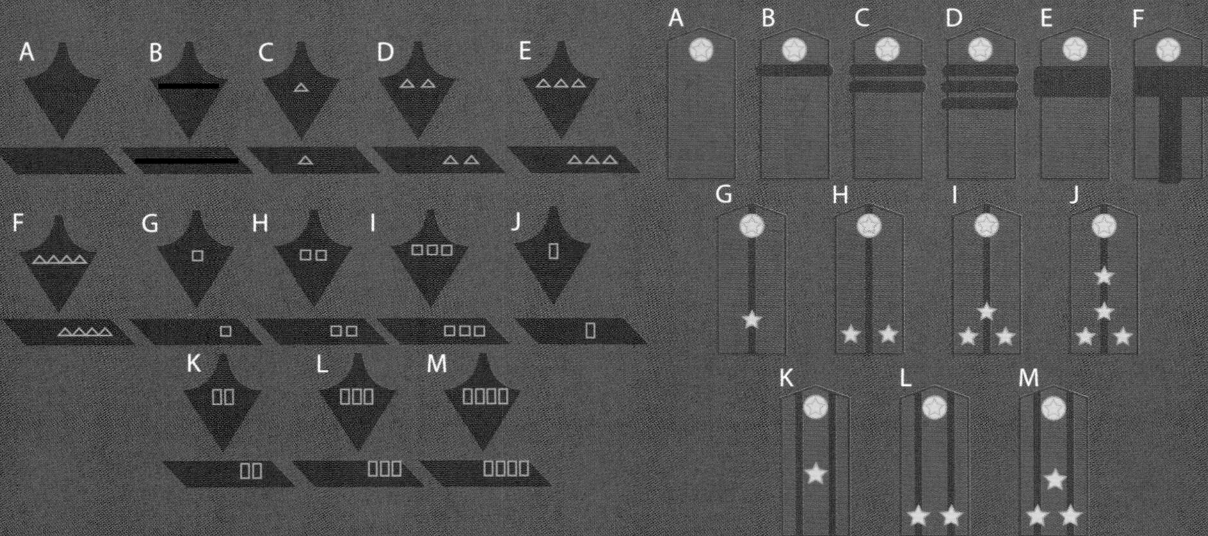

On the left Evgeny Zakharovich Blant wears an *obr* 43 *gimnastyorka* smock (no breast pockets), and on the right his friend wears a fully buttoned shirt. The *gimnastyorka* was produced in summer (cotton) and winter (wool) weights, the former fading and looking lighter, and the latter looking darker. Both men wear a *pilotka* cap and *sharovary* breeches. Their weapons are a PPSh-41 with a 71-round drum magazine (left), and a Mosin-Nagant M91/30. Blant was drafted, enlisted in the cavalry, and deployed to the front at the end of 1942. He took part in combat operations as an 82mm mortar operator, and during breaks between battles cooked for HQ officer staff. His regiment fought across Ukraine, Poland, and Hungary, and his last battles were fought near Dresden. *Blavatnik Archive*

Uniform

Undershirt and shorts or long johns were available in cotton (summer) or flannel (winter). Whether they were exchanged every ten days for cleaning depended on circumstances.

The tunic—*gimnastyorka*—used at the start of the war was the *obr* 1935. It had two breast pockets and a fall collar on which insignia were placed. In 1943 a major change took place with the arrival of the *obr* 1943 *gimnastyorka*, which had a two-buttoned, stand-up collar and shoulder boards. Officers' tunics had concealed breast pockets which, from 1944, were also used by NCOs and men. The summer issue was cotton; the winter issue was in wool. Both were worn with white linen collar liners (*podvorotnichok*) that were changed daily.

Breeches—*sharovary*—came in *obr* 35 and *obr* 43 versions, the former with buttons for braces; the latter with a narrower waistband and cloth loops for a belt although in practice the men sewed on buttons to allow their use. Knee patches can be seen in roughly 20 percent of cases.

The Red Army enters Bucharest in Romania. The soldier on the right has the Excellent Artillery Personnel pin badge (crossed cannon) and a Guards Army pin badge. The soldier on the left wears campaign medals—the Defense of Moscow, for example—and a Guards Army pin badge. Their *gimnastyorka* are *obr* 43 summer versions. *Fototeca online a comunismului românesc Fotografia #C105*

Above: Early war marching order. The wartime shot shows soldiers in Leningrad, October 1942. They are armed with SVT-38s whereas the reenactors have Mosin–Nagants. Note the prewar spade carrier on the man at right of wartime picture. Reenactor carries a *ranyets* M38 pack with *plashch-palatka* cape/shelter rolled around the top and its accessories, rope, poles, and stakes attached at the bottom. Note front and rear images showing equipment attached to belt including ration bag at rear, ammunition pouches, and gasmask bag. *Marco Crolla; Waralbum.ru; Marco Crolla*

Left: Senior lieutenant's tunics. The top two (1 and 2) are *gimnastyorka* of a senior lieutenant of infantry—note the field insignia on both tunics: 1. An *obr* 43 *gimnastyorka* with high collar, *pogony* and Guards division badge; 2. The earlier *obr* 35 *gimnastyorka* with drop collar and muted *pitlitsi*. The lower two (3 and 4) are those of an engineer: 3. The red and gold chevrons on an *obr* 35 tunic with *obr* 40 insignia; 4. Red chevrons *obr* 35. *Craig and Connor Palfrey*

Right: Summer uniform: *obr* M1943 *gimnastyorka* with high collar and *pogony*, ORs' belt, *pilotka*, *sharovary* and *kirva* boots. *Marco Crolla*

Footwear

Red Army soldiers rarely used socks, using foot cloths (*portyanki*) instead. Over these they wore ankle boots and puttees (designed to be used in summer) and high *sapogi* boots in winter—although in reality both were in use. While prewar boots were made from leather, often with birch oil worked into them to improve their water resistance, the wartime *sapogi* boots were made from "tarpaulin" invented in 1903–04 by Mikhail M. Pomortsev.

During the 1920s and 1930s *kirza* was developed, primarily by Alexander M. Khomutov and Ivan V. Plotnikov. The Red Army trialed boots with *kirza* SK uppers during 1939–40, and after this Plotnikov became the chief engineer for the supply of *kirza* SK boots to the army. John Gibbon:

> *Kirza* SK is a pig leather imitation based on multi-layer coarse cotton fabric, impregnated by a film-forming synthetic rubber type substance involving a vacuum manufacturing process, which produced a fabric that is impervious to water, yet with a breathable membrane to let air through. The name *kirza* is supposed to have derived from an

Britain and the United States each sent about 15 million pairs of ankle boots to Russia. Worn with puttees (black, gray or khaki) in the warmer months they were popular because their tightness prevented detritus from getting into the boot, dried quickly when wet, and meant the feet didn't sweat so much. The high boots were better suited to the winter months. Note the soldier's PPSh-41 SMG with its 71-round drum magazine. *Fototeca online a comunismului românesc Fotografia #C074*

A cobbler replacing the sole of a "tarpaulin" high boot. The early all-leather boot, the *yuft*, was highly prized because of its waterproof properties and flexibility. The ORs' *kirza* SK boots had moulded rubber soles, as seen in the photo. Our cobbler has the tools of his trade, wax and string, and his PPSh-41. *World War photos*

Soviet soldiers pass through liberated Polotsk, Belorussia (now Polatsk) on July 4, 1944. Note the ankle boots and putties rather than *sapogi* high boots. Mikhail Liderman remembers that "at the military school we were drilled to get up and wrap our puttees in forty seconds." *Unknown author/http://pohodd.ru/gal/v/Voennyj_albom/ot_kremly/0260/WikiCommons*

acronym from *KIRovsky ZAvod* (Kirov Plant), but the actual name of the factory where it was manufactured was the Iskozh Plant, Kirov Region (from *iskusstvennaya kozha*—artificial leather). To the troops they were simply known as "tarpaulin" boots or "shit trampers!"

Waist Belts (*remyon poyasnoy*)

These came in several forms. Those for officers originally had an open buckle embossed with a star and hammer and sickle (*obr* 35), were 50mm wide and were usually worn with a Sam Browne strap. Later in the war the buckle became a plain open version with two tines. Sergeants' belts were 45mm wide, with an open buckle, roller, and single tine. Other ranks' belts were 35mm wide, plain with an open buckle and a single tine. During the war an economy belt was made from webbing.

The Value of Equipment

Arkadiy Dayel recalls: "The guys in my unit knew, of course [that it was my birthday]. Back when we left for the front, we got a present from the queen of England: a green [uniform], good material, khaki in color. I think George VI was king at the time; all our clothing was of good quality and green—pants, tunics. And we had these great wide belts. My friends said to me: 'How shall we celebrate? We should drink!' But we didn't have anything; they hadn't brought any. But we knew that the drivers always had some alcohol stashed away. They took me over to one of the drivers who had brought in some food and ammunition. 'I can give you a flask of moonshine, but you have to take off your belt'—it was a great belt—'I'll give you a canvas belt [instead]. You're going to die anyway.' Just like that: 'You're going to die anyway. You're in the infantry; you'll go into battle and they'll kill you.' [He said this] without any embarrassment. 'Let's trade: I will give you this belt, and you give me your belt and also a towel. Do you have a towel?' I said, 'I have two towels.' 'Great. You keep one towel and give me the other.' That's how we got a flask of blue moonshine. I had no idea what that was. We got very sick from that moonshine, barely recovered from it. That's how I celebrated my eighteenth birthday at the front. I never forgot that moonshine. I've never touched moonshine again." (*BA*)

Officer *obr* 32 belt rig variants. At bottom left is the map case *obr* 32 with map insert (above center). The pistol is a TT30. *Craig and Connor Palfrey*

The future Belorussian writer Vasil Bykov in Romania in 1944 as a lieutenant. He wears an *obr* 43 double-breasted greatcoat with *pogony* and revised collar tabs. Note how the olive-gray tabs stand out from the background gray of the coat. Also note plain buckle belt and Sam Browne strap. *From Bykau.com/WikiCommons*

Overcoats and Winter Clothing

The *shinel'* (greatcoat) used at the start of the war was the *obr* 35, which had sleeve cuffs that could be turned down (the left cuff had a hidden pocket for a field dressing) and a collar that could be turned up. The *obr* 41 version wasn't as well made and lacked the cuffs. Officers' versions had buttons; ORs' coats fastened using four hooks and eyes. It was often carried as a *skatka*—a bedroll over the left shoulder (leaving the firing arm free). Sometimes it was wrapped up in the *plashch-palatka* cape/tent quarter. When rolled, it was often used to contain personal items. The coat was used as a blanket:

> We slept in the trenches. We used our overcoats as a pillow, as a blanket, as a sheet beneath us. How many overcoats did we have? Just one. Just one overcoat. We used our rucksacks as pillows. The rucksacks contained a waffle-cloth towel, a change of underwear, and a pair of footwraps to wrap around [our feet]. (*Arkadiy Dayel/BA*)

Hugely important and—compared to the Germans—in good supply in 1941–42, the Red Army's winter clothing started with the iconic *shapka-ushanka* (lit: earflap cap) fur cap. Officers' *ushankas* were made from wool or astrakhan, ORs' from a synthetic material. These replaced the *budyenovka* which wasn't effective in extreme temperatures.

Frontniks wearing a *telogreyka* (bodywarmer) padded jacket and padded trousers. Extremely effective cold weather gear, the jacket was also called a *vatnik*. An interesting footnote to this is the modern use of "*vatnik*" to mean a dyed-in-the-wool follower of the Russian government line, the implication being that such people have wooly brains. Both wartime soldier and reenactor carry the ubiquitous PPSh-41. At right, *valenki* boots. Note abandoned German 10.5cm leFH 18 light field howitzer and helmet in the Budapest scene. *Fortepan/Vörös Hadserag; Marco Crolla*

The M1941 *shinel'* greatcoat was made of heavy gray wool with a hook front instead of buttons, large collar, slash pockets at the waist, internal pocket, and back belt; it was cut to length. When not in use it was rolled up and worn over the non-firing shoulder, usually the left, with a strap securing the ends. Boris Stambler said: "These overcoat rolls were very uncomfortable. Whereas Germans carried their overcoats slung over their backs, we had ours rolled up. We rolled them up, strapped the ends together, and put them across our chests. They got in the way." *Marco Crolla*

The quilted jackets (*vatnaya telogreyka*) and trousers (*vatnaya sharovary*) entered service in 1935 but had been improved by the time that war started. The M41—and later the M43—had the same collar arrangement as the *gimnastyorka*, the M41 having belt loops and the M43 having a half-belt at the back for tightening. The *telogreyka* (body warmer) was supposed to be worn over the *gimnastyorka* and under the greatcoat but was often seen without the latter which restricted movement in combat. A woolen balaclava (*podshlemnik*) was used as were mittens (*rukavitsy*) with a firing finger, or gloves (*perchatki*). *Valenki* boots, made from compressed felt, were good in cold, dry conditions, but if it was, damp galoshes were necessary.

The other winter coat often seen in wartime photographs is the *bekesha* or *tulup* sheepskin coat with the fleece worn on the inside. It fastened with six big buttons and loops so that it could be done up/undone with mittens.

Camouflage Clothing

The Red Army was an early exponent of camouflage clothing. As early as 1919 the Soviets had initiated research and development and established a school for instruction on camouflage methods—or "masking." During the 1920s and 1930s they had developed and

The *bekesha* sheepskin coat was worn with the fleece inside. Issued from 1931, these coats were susceptible to infestation by lice. Mikhail Liderman remembers: "[We] were tormented by lice. It is difficult to convey what that is like. We would take our undershirts off and when we shook them, we could see the insects fall off. We decided to 'roast' them because it was early October [1943] and the weather was not yet too cold. ... We would take an empty gasoline barrel and put sticks and wooden boards at the bottom to separate things, put a little water in, and throw our uniforms in. We then lit a fire. The boiling water would do the 'roasting.'" These coats were sometimes called *tulup* or *shuba*. The shorter version of the coat was called a *polishubok*. *Marco Crolla*

Above: The snow camouflage suit came in two versions: hooded smock and trousers or a one-piece hooded smock that reached to the wearer's ankles which was fastened at the front by tie tapes and could be worn over the greatcoat. In the field, colored cloth armbands were worn to distinguish friend from foe, who might be similarly attired in winter camouflage. *Blavatnik Archive*

Above right: This soldier wears the SSh-40 helmet (six rivets on the lower exterior), and subdued *pitlitsi* showing the metal pip of a junior lieutenant. He wears the MKK amoeba brown on light green or khaki camouflage smock with a drawstring (at top) and hood (unseen). Tucked into his officer's belt (wider than ORs') with a stamped brass star, is an RGD-33 grenade without a fragmentation sleeve. *World War photos*

Right: Reenactor as a *Razvedchiki* (scout) wearing the M1941 summer leaf pattern, *Beryozka* (birch) MKK suit. He is armed with a PPS-43 SMG. *Marco Crolla*

A Soviet sniper wearing a *Mochalniy* camouflage suit in Karelia, 1941. The British called them ghillie suits and similarly used jute thread, hessian, or strips of burlap along with natural greenery. The modern reenactor version uses dyed raffia. *Sa-Kuva; Simon Vanlint*

introduced various personal camouflage clothing and several other aids for field camouflage such as portable screens, fringes, and netting etc.

During the war the Germans produced several reports on Soviet camouflage and concealment practices to inform their own troops and to allow their forces to adopt similar practices. It was generally acknowledged that the Soviets were far more adept than the Germans on the subject.

Available in hooded two-piece (MKK—*Maskirovochniy Kamuflirovanniy Kostyum*) or coverall (MK—*Maskirovochniy Kombinezon*) forms, the Red Army had a range of camouflaged clothing from sandy colors through various greens and browns to winter white and in varying disruptive patterns and shapes, including initially the distinctive "amoeba" splotch patterns and the later printed leaf/foliage and block patterns developed during the war. Each reflected use in the respective terrains and seasons. The amoeba pattern alone had 12 known color patterns. They were issued to snipers, scouts, combat engineers, and reconnaissance troops. In the field, colored cloth armbands were worn to distinguish friendly from enemy units, who could be similarly attired in winter camouflage clothing.

Equipment

The photographs over the following pages show the range of packs, ammunition pouches, water canteens, entrenching shovels, gasmask bags etc that were used by the Red Army.

About 900,000 women served in the Red Army and many were in combat units, enduring the same deprivations as the men. They fought as tank and armored vehicle crews, medics, artillerists, and, most famously, as snipers. There were also all-women Army Air Force regiments, the "Night Witches." The soldier in the photograph wears a *pilotka* cap and the *gimnastyorka* but tailored to fit and with reversed fly-front. The breeches (*sharovary*) have knee patches and her boots are *sapogi* of (tarpaulin) synthetic rubber, the most common of all high boots. Her rolled overcoat is over her shoulder, and she carries the SSh-39 helmet (three external rivets) and an *obr* 40 medical bag minus the Red Cross. *World War photos*

Soviet sailors marching in Leningrad, less than a month into the siege that would last 872 days. These troops carry Mosin–Nagants with fixed bayonets, gasmask bags on their left sides, and some carry the shapeless *veshchmeshok* packs. *ww2dbase Russian International News Agency Boris Kudoyarov*

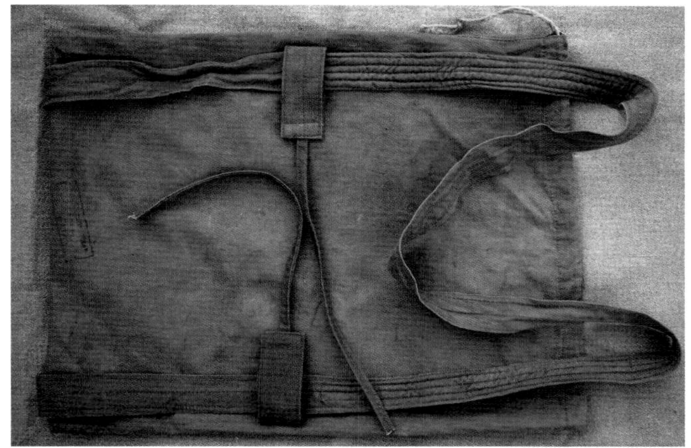

An M42 pack (*veshchmeshok*). The larger Model 1930—up to 65cm x 43cm—had a wooden toggle fastener in one corner. Other more complicated packs came out in 1936, 1939, and 1941, but after hostilities started, the simple, quick-and-cheap-to-produce sack-type pack was redesigned and introduced some time in 1942—as here, which measures roughly 42cm x 51cm. *Simon Vanlint*

A selection of an enlisted man's personal wartime items to go in the *veshchmeshok obr* 41 backpack: (1) notebook, (2) sewing kit and personal documents, (3) toothbrush, (4) paper tobacco packets with red smoking pouch, (5) and (6) two types of mess tin, both standard throughout the war years, (7) mug that fits inside the *obr* 36 mess tin (6), (8) various food packets, (9) *plashch-palatka* shelter half/rain cape (manual says to store in *meshok* or across body in a roll). *Craig and Connor Palfrey*

Above: Front and back of *ranyets* backpacks. Left: officer's *obr* 38; right: enlisted man's prewar *obr* 36. *Craig and Connor Palfrey*

Below: A selection of mess items: (1) The big round model 1924 mess tin. This is often referred to as a three-man mess tin, as up to three soldiers were expected to share from it. (2) Three mugs, two enameled and a smaller aluminum cup. The latter isn't genuine, it's a reproduction *starshina* cup (*starshina* = sergeant-major). It was his responsibility to organize the vodka ration, and this small mug is the one used to measure the ration. Viktor Ginzberg remembers: "our sergeant-major was a very crafty Ukrainian, he managed to receive vodka for both the dead and the wounded as well. We each got a whole glass. The soldiers would line up in front of his thermos and he would pour a glass of vodka for each of us. We drank it and then walked for half a kilometer to our field kitchen." (*BA*) (3) Restored *obr* 36 mess tin set. All mess tins and metal canteens were left as bare metal until 1940 when they were painted green, so you can find older models still in storage being painted green before being issued after 1940! (4) Genuine spoons, from left: two standard issue spoons, one with a hole punched in the handle, another with the owner's name punched on; the next two are trench art spoons, and the last is an issue teaspoon, most likely only found in barrack canteens for officers etc. Soldiers called up after hostilities had started were often told to bring their own spoon and cup, and as early as 1933 a standardized wooden spoon was approved. This not only saved metal but did not freeze to the lips, as had happened with spoons issued during the Winter War. Some units had such shortages that workshops were set up to manufacture items from any available metal, often from food tins, cups made from Lend-Lease tin cans, which were quite common, kettles and water dispensers from gasmask filters. (5) The aluminum bowl is also a genuine battlefield dig-up, restored in St. Petersburg. Enamel bowls were also known to have been used. *Simon Vanlint*

A look of eager anticipation as cooks await the warrant officer's approval. A soldier's spoon was often the personal item which he valued over anything else: it was the individual's own; it didn't belong to the state. As one soldier wrote, "without a spoon, just as without a rifle, it is impossible to wage war." Many were wooden, but many were aluminum—easier to mark than wood, and many were etched with messages, milestones in life and dates. Abram Kotlyar remembers: "A military kitchen traveled with us. We had a large cauldron and the kitchen poured porridge or soup or something else into it. And we would sit together, 10 or 15 of us, and each one would reach into [the cauldron] with his own spoon. Those that had wooden spoons were lucky. Those who had metallic spoons, and if you had to drink with it, well, you can imagine what those poor souls would get with a small metallic spoon. Also, of course, we were given pieces of bread." *NAC*

Personal equipment pictured on an issue towel. Everything is genuine except the mirror. The issue mirror was small and round and had a tortoiseshell-style edge. The mirrors were also inserted inside discarded gasmask lens frames. *Simon Vanlint*

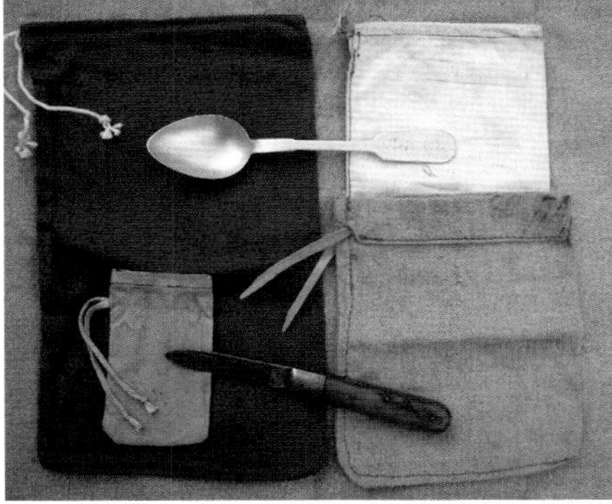

Soldiers were not issued a knife or fork because of shortages. Pocket knives were popular at the time, so most soldiers had one. The spoon is the standard issue with a soldier's name punched onto it. The bags are genuine ration bags. *Simon Vanlint*

A selection of water bottles and covers. *Craig and Connor Palfrey*

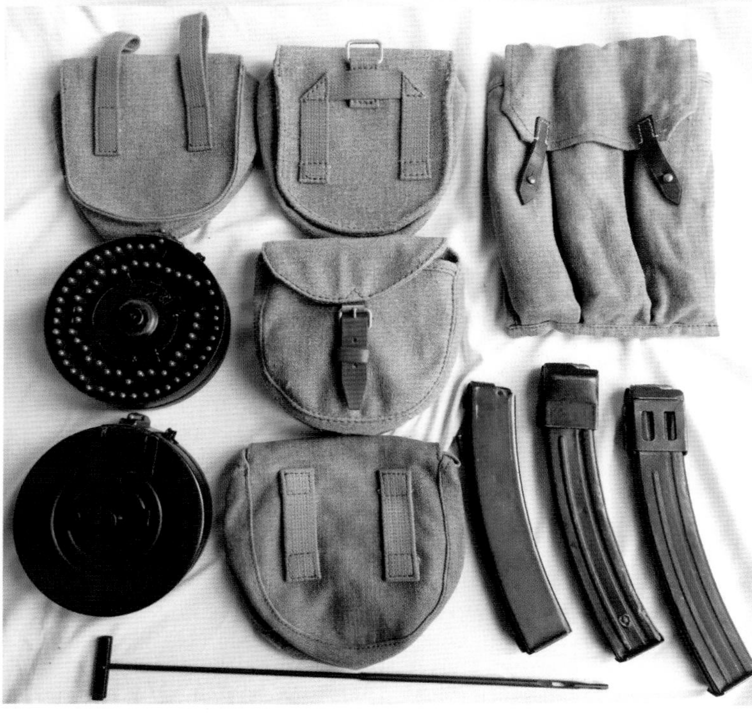

Submachine-gun ammunition storage. Variants of drum magazine pouch for the PPSh-41. Top center was designed for the PPD40 but widely used for PPSh magazines in the early war period as they were the same size. At left, the 71-round magazine with and without cover removed. At right, a variant of pouch for PPSh stick magazines and three stick mags: left, for the PPS43 SMG center, a 1942 model magazine for the PPSh. This type was short-lived and superseded from 1943 by the far-right magazine. Manufacture of the 1942 magazine stopped because its thin sides easily dented and stopped it from feeding. At bottom, an SMG cleaning rod. *Craig and Connor Palfrey*

Grenade bags. The dark gray bag carries genuine vintage RGD-33 grenades, and two fuses wrapped in brown paper in the internal pocket (modern dummy reproductions). The other bag contains 3 x F-1 and 1 x RTD-42 grenades with transport plugs in place. The fuses are carried separately in the internal pocket. These grenades and fuses are Cold War era. Many reenactors use a smaller three-cell grenade pouch. While this is an item true to the period, it was usually mounted inside tanks—although it could be worn on the belt by the tank crew if their vehicle was disabled and the crew continued on foot. *Simon Vanlint*

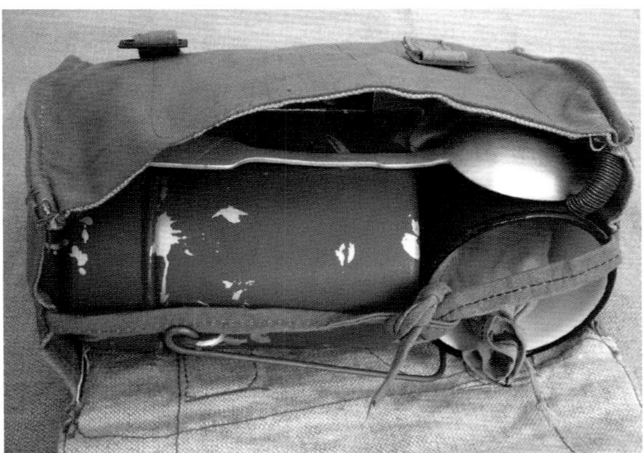

The 1941 produce bag was introduced that year, and canceled shortly thereafter. Those available today are often from storage depots as not many were issued. They were to be used in conjunction with the models 1939 and 1941 rucksacks, as these were quite small. The contents are genuine, although the mess tins were recovered from a battlefield dig around St. Petersburg and have been workshop restored and painted. *Simon Vanlint*

A 1940-dated model 1940 gasmask bag made of cotton duck. The simplified version is made of soft cotton twill with wooden toggles, and simplified waist tie instead of a strap with buckle. There were numerous variants of the model 1940 from 1942 onwards differing in manufacturing details. Today, these are often referenced as the model 1942, but technically it wasn't a new model, just a simplified economy version of the model 1940. There were other older models in use from 1936 and 1938, but they were not so common. *Simon Vanlint*

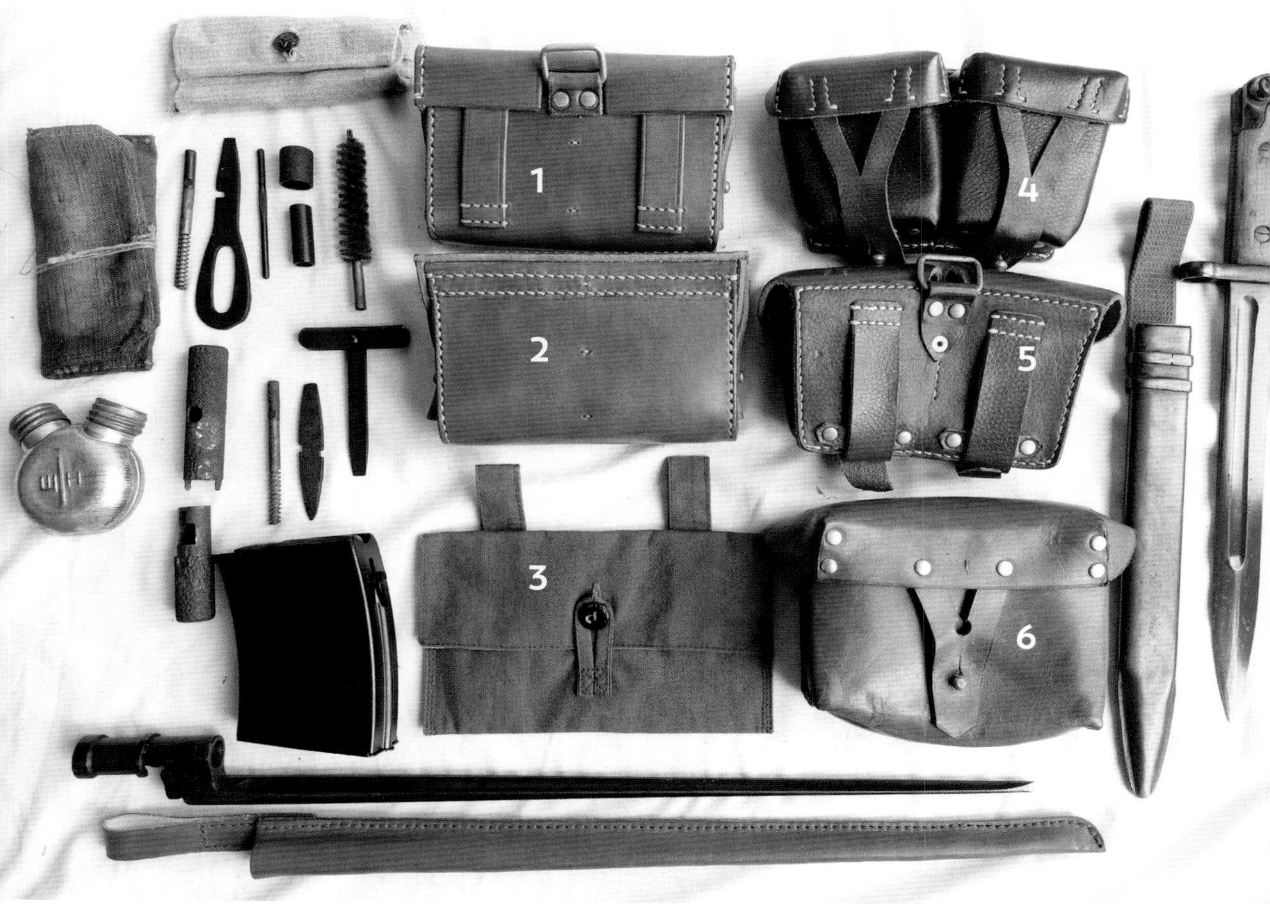

At left, cleaning kits issued to each soldier: the beige one is for the SVT-40; green is for Mosin–Nagants. The silver container has half oil, half cleaning solution. Most notable is the metal tube in two pieces, which is the container for the 1937 cleaning kit produced at the Batishchev plant. It doubled up as a tool—one end slotted onto the end of the barrel to guide in the cleaning rod; the other end became a handle for the screwdriver. In 1941 the factory stopped production of the tube container, replacing it with the simplified set in green canvas. Below the cleaning kits is a 10-round SVT-40 magazine and at the very bottom is a bayonet for the M91/30 with a prewar scabbard.

The pouches: (1) and (2) *obr* 37 rifle pouches front and back—essentially imperial-style pouches but with a hoop to allow them to be attached to the *obr* 36 backpack. (3) green universal ammunition pouch, designed to be worn below the leather pouch so a soldier could carry additional ammunition. (4) and (5) leather M91/30 pouches *obr* 37 model (standard wartime issue). (6) SVT 38/40 pouch designed to house either mags or stripper clips.

Ammunition pouches were originally made of leather either as a single pouch like the cloth version or as two-section pouches. Other materials—even wood—were also used. In 1941 some were produced with the front made of *kirza* (artificial leather made from cotton fabric coated with plastic). The introduction of the SVT-38 and -40 led to leather pouches that could hold two magazines. From 1941 these were discontinued and replaced by a pouch—versions were made from made from real and artificial leather or canvas—to carry either Mosin–Nagant clips or SVT magazines. During the war a simplified version came in that could take clips or a single SVT magazine. At right, an SVT-40 bayonet and scabbard. *Craig and Connor Palfrey*

Typical equipment assembly as shown in Soviet instruction manuals: (1) Standard rifleman's kit—rifle ammo pouches, grenade bag, ration bag, water bottle, spade, ammo pouches; (2) Standard SMG kit; (3) and (4) PPD gunner with three/two magazine pouches. *EF*

Right: Reenactors wearing *telogreyka* padded jackets, with *plashch-palatka* roll across body. The man at left has an ammunition bandoleer, puttees and carries a Model 1944 carbine with folding bayonet. The man at right carries a PPSh-41 SMG and wears *kirza* boots. *Marco Crolla*

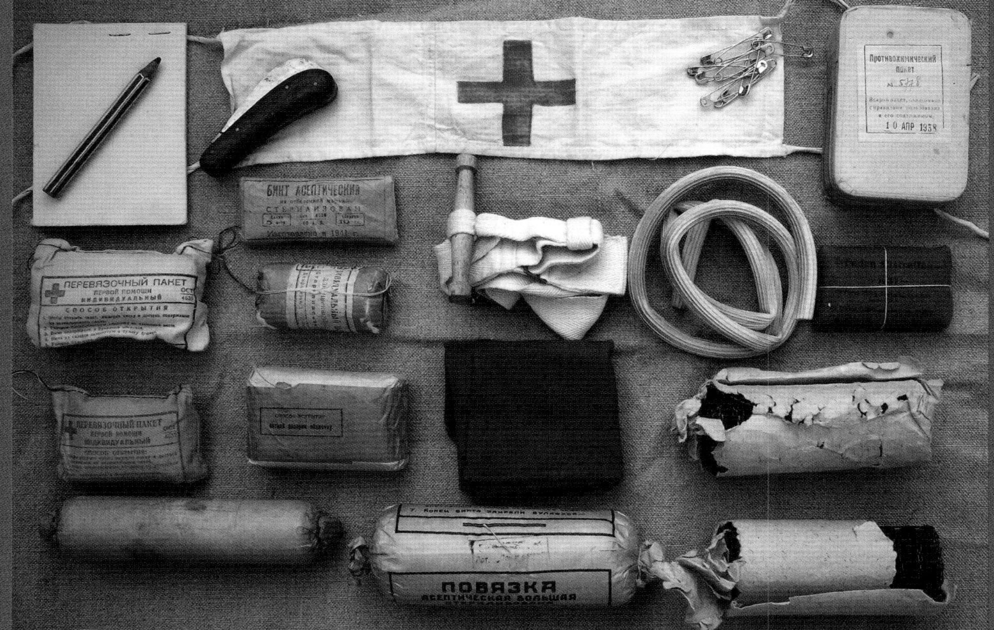

1938 Medical Bag Contents

Item	*Description*	*Quantity*	*Compartment*
1	Ammonia spirit in ampoules 0.5–1.0 KS each (in cases)	10 each	1
2	Iodine tincture in ampoules 0.5–1.0 KS each (in cases)	10 each	1
3	Soft gauze bandages 10cm wide x 5m long	5 each	2–4
4	First aid bandage packs	5 each	20–24
5	Small antiseptic dressings	5 each	16–18
6	Kerchiefs for bandages	3	9–13
7	Safety pins 4–4.5cm	20	Flap
8	Haemostatic cloth tourniquets	3	5, 25, 26
9	Metal mesh splints	2	15
10	Medium straight scissors	1	7
11	Folding garden knife	1	14
12	Individual chemical pack T-D-2	1	19
13	Notebook	1	27
14	Chemical pencil	1	27

Photo shows a medic's armband and examples of the items officially carried. All items shown are originals including a captured German dressing. Later, Lend-Lease items were carried. A law was passed late in 1941 declaring that everything on the battlefield was state property, and that removing anything without permission was a court-martial offense. Everything of use was reused by the state: weapons, food, vehicles, fuel, clothing, and equipment was all gathered up by quartermasters and sorted for redistribution. German fabric was often used for backing on insignia, or lining in clothing, etc.

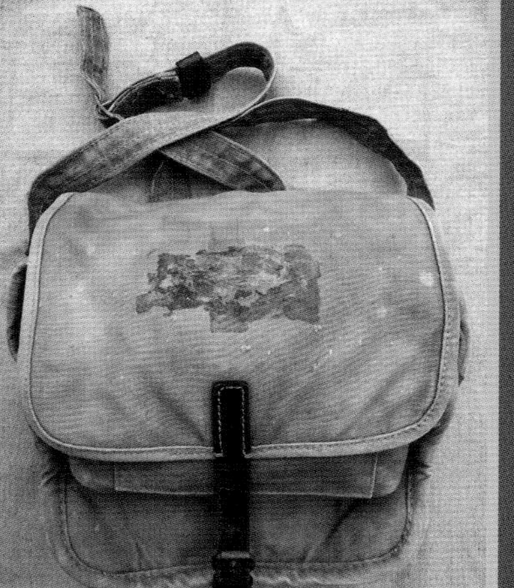

The *obr* 36 medical bag had leather trim to the flap and body. From 1940 (as here) they were made as a slightly simplified version with cotton tape trim. Both bags had 28 numbered compartments, and the medical manuals contained a list of what was supposed to be carried, the quantities and in which of the numbered pockets each item should be carried. Each soldier was supposed to carry a field dressing, and had basic training on how to apply it; medics were supposed to use a soldier's own dressing where possible, and recover unused dressings from the dead. *All Simon Vanlint*

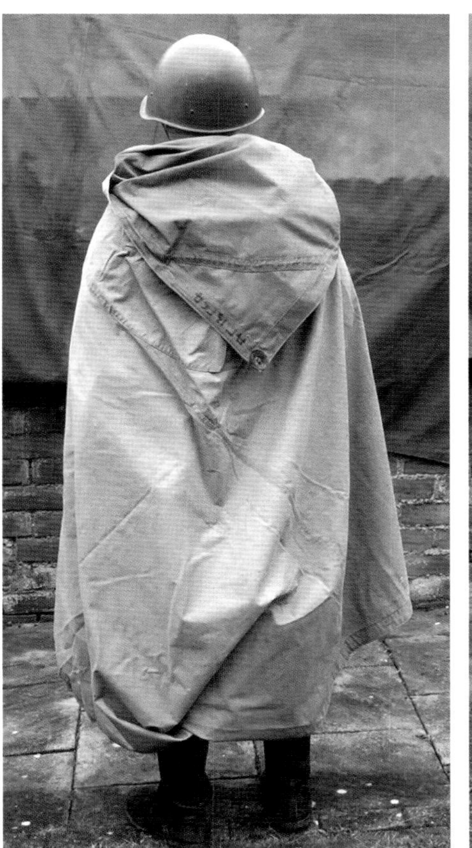

PPSh-41-armed reenactor wearing a *plashch-palatka* as a rain cape. *Marco Crolla*

1940-dated *plashch-palatka*, with all the accessories on top. Note the sewn grommets and braided tie—everything original except the rope, which is probably modern. There were two styles of carry bags for the pole set, but they were only ever issued with the models 1939 and 1941 rucksacks; for other packs they were carried inside the pack and did not need a special bag. *Simon Vanlint*

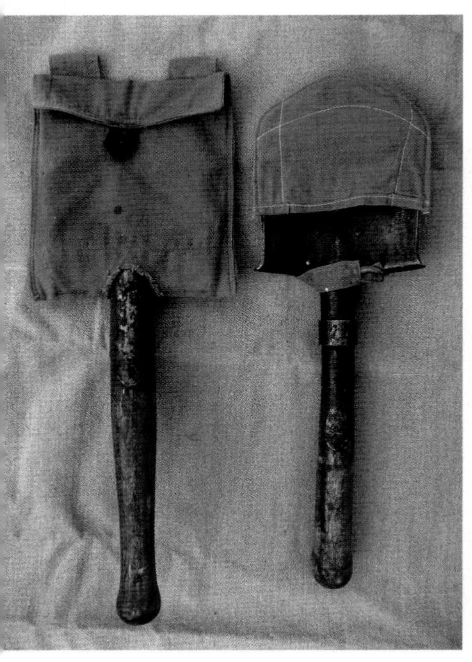

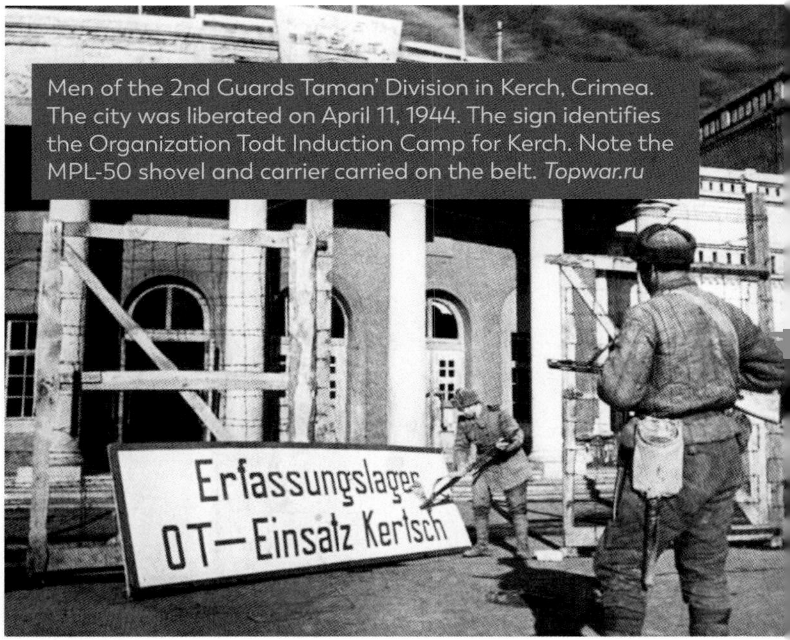

Men of the 2nd Guards Taman' Division in Kerch, Crimea. The city was liberated on April 11, 1944. The sign identifies the Organization Todt Induction Camp for Kerch. Note the MPL-50 shovel and carrier carried on the belt. *Topwar.ru*

Entrenching tool covers: prewar (left) and wartime. The prewar covers were normally full covers (as here). After hostilities started, they got simpler, using less fabric, undyed or even with alternative dark colors such as gray, secured by cheap metal buttons or wooden toggles. There were two distinct types of tool: one with a flat blade, the other pointed. In 1944 the flat blade version was canceled, and a new simplified version of the pointed blade tool became standard: the MPL-50 (*Malaya Pekhotnaya Lopata*—small infantry shovel—with a length of 50cm. Both this and the large sapper's shovel BSL-110 (*Bol'shaya Sapernaya Lopata* 110cm long) were also used as measuring devices for digging trenches and defenses etc. They had many other uses: paddle, frying pan, and a close-quarter fighting weapon, for example. *Simon Vanlint*

Rifle Division Manpower 1939–45

Date	*Total men*	*Date*	*Total men*
September 13, 1939	18,841	July 28, 1942	10,566
April 5, 1941	14,454	December 12, 1942	9,447
July 29, 1941	10,790	December 1942 Guards Division	10,556
December 6, 1941	11,907	June 1944–May 1945	9,619
March 18, 1942	12,813		

The big change in numbers between 1939 and July 1941 was because of losing the light tank battalion, howitzer artillery regiment, and the mechanized reconnaissance elements, and an overall reduction in service units—the divisional hospital, for example, was taken over by the army. TM 30-430 summed up the 1945 rifle division:

> the forward firepower of the rifle division has been increased by a generous allotment to the rifle regiments of submachine guns, machine guns, and mortars. Thus, … as compared with the 1939 rifle division, [it] has a reduced reconnaissance ability and weaker replacement capacity, but it has better tactical and strategic mobility. With normal artillery attachment, it has greater firepower.

Basic Rifle Division Weapons

Table of Organisation and Equipment: Rifle Division

Unit	Men	7.62mm rifle	7.62mm SMG	7.62mm LMG	7.62mm HMG	12.7mm AAMG	14.5mm ATR	50mm mor	82mm mor	120mm mor	45mm ATG
HQ & HQ Co	117	110	6	1	–	–	–	–	–	–	–
Ren Tr	74	–	68	6	–	–	–	–	–	–	–
Sig Co	130	90	40	–	–	–	–	–	–	–	–
Engr Bn	164	149	15	–	–	–	–	–	–	–	–
CW's Co	40	25	15	–	–	–	–	–	–	–	–
Div Arty Regt	998	738	206	18	–	–	36	–	–	–	–
AT Bn, Mtz	233	172	43	6	–	–	18	–	–	–	12
AAMG Co, Mtz	97	67	30	–	–	18	–	–	–	–	–
Repl Co	100	75	25	5	–	–	2	2	2	–	2
Med Bn	90	90	–	–	–	–	–	–	–	–	–
Vet Hosp	11	11	–	–	–	–	–	–	–	–	–
Bakery	63	63	–	–	–	–	–	–	–	–	–
Trans Co	80	80	–	–	–	–	–	–	–	–	–
3 R Regts	7,422	3,756	1,950	486	135	–	162	54	81	21	36
Total	9,619	5,426	2,398	522	135	18	218	56	83	21	50

Unit	76mm How	76mm Gun	122mm How	Tractor	Trailer	Truck	Sp veh	Horse veh	Horse	Kitchen	Radio
HQ & HQ Co	–	–	–	–	–	–	5	–	25	1	2
Ren Tr	–	–	–	–	–	–	–	–	80	–	2
Sig Co	–	–	–	–	–	–	2	20	29	1	7
Engr Bn	–	–	–	–	–	4	–	9	18	1	2
CW's Co	–	–	–	–	–	2	6	10	–	1	
Div Arty Regt	–	24	12	21	12	10	17	99	587	11	16
AT Bn, Mtz	–	–	–	–	–	39	–	–	–	2	11
AAMG Co, Mtz	–	–	–	–	–	18	–	–	–	–	–
Repl Co	–	–	–	–	–	–	–	5	10	–	–
Med Bn	–	–	–	–	–	9	–	25	31	1	–
Vet Hosp	–	–	–	–	–	–	–	2	2	–	–
Bakery	–	–	–	–	–	3	–	–	–	–	–
Trans Co	–	–	–	–	–	54	–	–	–	1	–
3 R Regts	12	–	–	–	–	21	42	444	981	45	15
Total	12	24	12	21	12	160	66	610	1,773	63	56

This table shows the establishment and weaponry for a 1944–45 rifle division. The numbers of personnel changed during the war as indicated below—but the totals are academic. At very few stages during the period 1939–45 were divisions at anywhere near full strength—and if they were it wasn't for long. There were shortages of weapons and, of course, a huge attrition rate on manpower. Nevertheless, the table—and accompanying photos—give an idea of the weapons used. A few points to note: (a) the 45mm antitank guns were replaced where possible by 57mm and even 76mm guns; (b) the number of horses gives away the fact that the division was primarily horse-drawn; (c) the replacement company of 100 men means that attrition reduces the effectiveness of the division quickly; (d) Guards rifle regiments tended to be larger than ordinary ones; (e) finally, TM 30-430 highlights the fact that:

> Although the personnel strength of the Red Army rifle division is 4,424 smaller than the U.S. infantry division, its combat strength is only 200 less. Its supporting and service elements make up only 26 and 12 percent of its total strength, respectively, as compared with 36 and 21 percent in the U.S. infantry division.

The five men above and the reenactor (right) are wearing SN-42 (steel bib) two-piece body armor. Made from 2mm (.08-inch) steel and weighing 3.35kg (7.7lb), it gave a degree of protection from small shrapnel fragments, bayonet thrusts, 9mm pistol rounds with lead cores and MP-38/40 rounds from 100 to 150 meters. When an iron core 9mm was adopted, the plates were thickened to 2.6mm and designated SN-46. There were mixed feelings about performance, with the plate performing well in street fighting and at close quarters, but being considered a burden in the field, especially when prone. Note the lack of plate on the right shoulder, the DP-27 LMG, and the amoeba-patterned overalls. *SF collection; Marco Crolla*

Above and below right: The PTRS-41 had a five-round magazine. *Greene Media Ltd; SF collection*

Use of antitank rifles against armored vehicles dropped off during the war as armor thickness increased and side skirts reduced the likelihood of spalling or side penetration. In 1942, antitank rifle companies in rifle regiments consisted of three platoons, giving a total of 27 PTRS or PTRD rifles. In 1942, companies armed with 16 antitank rifles were established at the infantry battalion level—these weapons were distributed into two platoons (four squads of two guns) but these were reduced in size in July 1942 to a solitary platoon of nine guns (three in three squads), because their effectiveness had dropped significantly. The Guards rifle regiment was reorganized in December 1942 to have a 1942-style antitank rifle company with 16 guns.

The PTRD-41 14.5mm single-shot antitank rifle. *Marco Crolla*

Mine Warfare

The U.S. Army's handbook on the Red Army notes:

> The Soviet Army placed so much importance on mine warfare that special mine units of up to battalion size were organized and employed in World War II. Unlike many armies, the Soviet Army teaches field improvisation of mines and the employment of captured mines. German combat reports state that the average Soviet combat soldier is adept in the use of mine warfare equipment and is particularly ingenious in installing improvised mines and booby traps. ... During World War II the Soviets used about 15 models of standard metallic and nonmetallic antitank mines, at least 15 models of antivehicular and antitransport mines, about 10 standard dual-purpose mines, and about 12 standard models of anti-personnel mines, as well as numerous improvised types and vast numbers of captured mines.

We've all heard the tales of Soviet penal battalions forced to walk across minefields to clear them. Unlike so much Western anti-communist rhetoric, this has a kernel of truth hidden away, as evinced by no less a source than President Dwight Eisenhower who reported a conversation with Zhukov:

> Highly illuminating to me was his description of the Russian method of attacking through mine fields. The German mine fields, covered by defensive fire, were tactical obstacles that caused us [the Western Allies] many casualties and delays. It was always a laborious business to break through them, even though our technicians invented every conceivable mechanical appliance to destroy mines safely. Marshal Zhukov gave me a matter-of-fact statement of his practice, which was, roughly, "There are two kinds of mines; one is the personnel mine and the other is the vehicular mine. When we come to a mine field our infantry attacks exactly as if it were not there. The losses we get from personnel mines we consider only equal to those we would have gotten from machine guns and artillery if the Germans had chosen to defend that particular area with strong bodies of troops instead of with mine fields. The attacking infantry does not set off the vehicular mines, so after they have penetrated to the far side of the field they form a bridgehead, after which the engineers come up and dig out the channels through which our vehicles can go."

In fact, the Red Army methods of mine clearing were similar to everyone else's. However, they often used artillery to clear gaps through known minefields, assisted by the fact that the German *Tellermines* were subject to sympathetic detonation because of the large area of their pressure plates. The Germans had less success with this method, because most of the Soviet field-improvised mines didn't have large pressure plates.

The Red Army used two main detectors: the VIM-203 and -210. Designed in 1939 the VIM-210 high-frequency mine detector M1939 used the Mosin–Nagant M91/30 as a carrier for the rectangular detection coil. It could detect the German TMi35 antitank *Tellermine* at 40–45 centimeters (up to 17.7 inches). All in all, around 250,000 of all types were produced.

The detector was attached to a wooden or plastic rod. The working parts were in a haversack which transmitted signals via headphones. The sappers would usually form a line with each being about 3–5 meters apart. A detected mine was marked, and a clear-up party removed it. *World War photos*

Left and below: The Degtyaryova Pekhotny LMG came in a variety of forms. First was the DP-27/DP-28, the standard Soviet infantry LMG of the war. Developed and introduced in the late 1920s, some 795,000 were produced. It fired the same 7.62×54mm rimmed round as the Mosin–Nagant—a significant help when it came to resupply. Weight was 9.12kg (20.11lb) unloaded. Gas-operated, with a 550rpm rate of fire, it had a 47-round, circular, clockwork-operated, pan-type magazine. *RIAN archive 58228 Vsevolod Tarasevich/WikiCommons (CC BY-SA 3.0); Greene Media Ltd*

Above: The main variant of the DP-27 was the DPM with a pistol grip. *Greene Media Ltd*

Left: DP-27 gunner using a portable (note the carrying handles) "sniper" shield, although this is something of a contradiction in terms—a sniper wouldn't advertise his presence with something so obvious—these were sometimes useful in static trench systems. The number 2 was there to assist in changing magazines as well as covering the flanks. *Michael Trakhman/albumwar2.com*

Below: The DT LMG was a tank-mounted weapon that could be detached and used as an assault weapon. The DP was modified to accommodate a ball mounting for tank use. The magazine was smaller but deeper to take more rounds than the DP—63 as opposed to 47. *Greene Media Ltd*

Right: The DShK 1938 12.7×108mm HMG was designed by Degtyaryov, modified by Shpagin, and entered production in 1938. Some 9,000 were produced at Tula Arms. A machine gun that packs a real punch, at 500 meters the DShK can penetrate up to 15mm of armor. It was used mainly on armored vehicles and less by the infantry who used it on a trolley with a small armored shield. It was also used in the AA role—the two-wheeled trolley could be converted into a tripod. It was heavy—the gun alone weighed 34kg (74lb 15oz), and combined with its wheeled mount it weighed 157kg (346lb). Its rate of fire was 600rpm to a max range of 2,500m (2,700yd). Its crew comprised gunner and spotter/loader, but more people were needed to carry ammunition that usually came from 50-round belts from a box. Note the AA spiderweb sights. *World War photos*

Right and below right: *Pulemyot Maxima* PM1910/30 (Maxim's machine gun) 7.62×54R HMG was introduced in 1910, a derivation of Hiram Maxim's original weapon. Between 1910 and 1945 some 176,000 were produced within the State Armories and later the State Arsenals. The Sokolov mount gave good traverse and made the weapon more mobile over anything other than rough ground when its heavy weight meant—as this photograph of a Finnish squad with two weapons shows—a team was needed to carry it and the ammunition. Water-cooled, it weighed 62.66kg (138.1lb) and fired at 600rpm from a 250-round canvas belt to an effective range of 1,500m (1,640yd) to 3,500m (3,800yd) max. It was replaced by the Goryunov SG-43. *NAC; Greene Media Ltd*

Left: The Goryunov SG-43 air-cooled, gas-operated MMG was introduced in 1943. Manufactured at the Kovrov plant, it replaced the PM1910, weighed 120kg (266lb), and had a chromium-lined, removable heavy barrel. Firing 500–700rpm to an effective range of 1,100m (1,200yd), it was wheel-mounted with a shield. The mounting could be tilted to allow use in the AA role. *Greene Media Ltd*

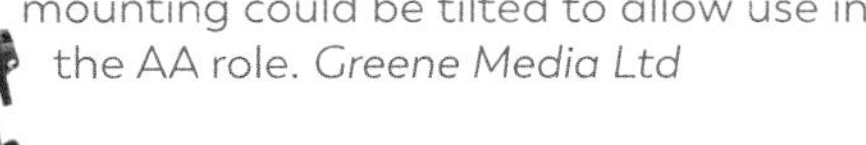

Above: Typical weapons carried by the Soviet infantryman. Top: Two PPD-40 SMGs. The PPD (*Pistolet-Pulemyot Degtyaryova* = Degtyaryov's machine pistol) was designed in 1934 and produced in small numbers until 1940 when over 80,000 were made. Officially replaced by the PPSh-41, it fired a 7.62×25mm Tokarev pistol cartridge from a 25-round box magazine (replaced by a 71-round drum magazine). Middle: A sheath, two clockwork, 71-round drum 7.62mm magazines with a wristwatch on top, and four RDG-33 hand-grenades without fragmentation sleeves. Bottom: Binoculars, a handpump torch, Tokarev TT-30 semiautomatic pistol, an aluminum water-bottle, and a Finnish Puukko general-purpose knife and sheath. *SA-kuva*

Right: Created as a response to the Red Army's need for a cheaper version of the PPSh-41, the PPS—*Pistolet-pulemyot Sudayeva* (Sudayev's SMG)—could be produced with only 2.7 hours' machining and 6.2kg of steel (the PPSh-41 needed 13.9kg). Full-scale production of the PPS-43 (the improved version of the PPS-42) began in 1943. Over two million were made. It used the 7.62×25mm Tokarev M1930 pistol cartridge, fired at a rate of 500–600rpm to an effective range of 100–150m. *Greene Media Ltd*

Left: The *Pistolet-pulemyot Shpagina*-41 (Shpagin's machine-pistol-41) replaced the PPD in 1941. Some six million were produced in a production period from 1941 to 1947 (some five million during the war). It fired a 7.62×25mm Tokarev pistol cartridge from a 71-round drum (usually filled to no more than 65) or 35-round curved box. It had an effective range of 150–200m and a rate of fire of 900–1,000rpm. The Germans rechambered it for use with the standard German 9×19mm SMG ammunition or used Mauser ammunition which was the same size but underpowered. *Greene Media Ltd*

Nearly 20 million of the 91/30 were produced in the period. The name "3-line" stems from the old Russian "line" measurement, where 1 line = one tenth of an inch = 2.54mm. 3 lines, therefore, equals 7.62mm, the caliber we use today. *Greene Media Ltd*

A carbine of the 91/30 was produced in 1938—the M38—which became the M44 when a folding bayonet was attached (as here). Few of these were used on the Eastern Front. *Greene Media Ltd*

The SVT-38 semiautomatic—*Samozaryadnaya Vintovka Tokareva* (Tokarev self-loading rifle of 1938)—was produced from 1939 but proved difficult to maintain and was inaccurate over 600m. The SVT-40 (**1**) was an upgraded and improved version developed and introduced in 1940. Although built in large numbers—around 1,600,000 of which over 50,000 were the sniper version (**2**)—many were lost in the opening weeks of *Barbarossa* and cheaper submachine guns were preferred as replacements. The SVT-40 weighed 3.85kg (8.5lb) unloaded, and fired a 7.62×54mm R cartridge from a 10-round, detachable box magazine. With a PU x3.5 magnification scope modeled on the German Zeiss design, its effective range was 1,000m (1,100yd). In service the SVT-40 proved complex, unreliable, and difficult to maintain. Mikhail Liderman remembered: "After spending a few weeks in Liski we were issued weapons. We were issued new rifles, which were, by the way, SVTs, self-loading Tokarev rifles. These rifles are only good for parades. Those of us who have used them during the war know what they are like. They are very capricious weapons. If so much as a speck of dust got into the breechblock, the weapon would not fire ... When we were advancing after Kharkov, the SVT rifles became unusable, so it was hard to be in combat conditions. Many [soldiers] began getting rid of theirs by basically throwing them into a lake or whatever, and instead taking our old 3-line rifles which could fire under any conditions. If some sand got in, you could just "blow and spit," as we said at the front, and the breechblock would function, but the other one was very difficult. And those rifles, I don't know how many but there were probably a lot produced, they were all eventually scrapped." *Greene Media Ltd; TopGunRMNP/WikiCommons (CC-BY-SA 3.0)*

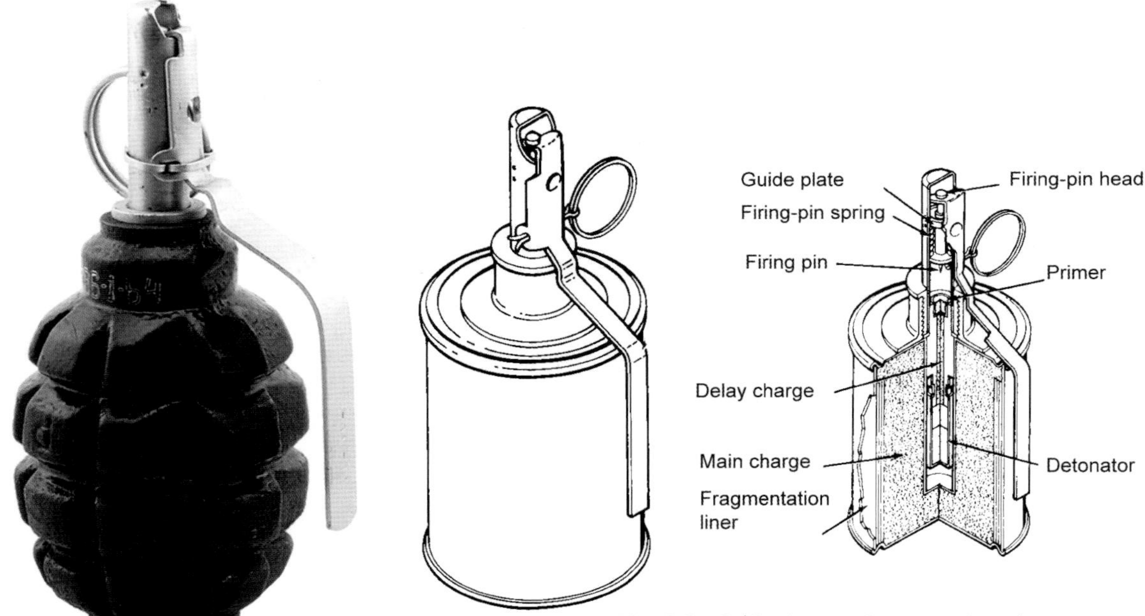

The F1 *Limonka* (lemon) fragmentation defensive grenade had a wide blast area. It had a 3.5- to 4-second fuse but this was adjustable for instant (boobytraps) or delayed action. *Stanislav S. Yanchenko/ WikiCommons (CC-BY-SA 3.0)*

The RG-42 (*Ruchnaya Granata* = hand grenade) was designed by S. G. Korshunov to replace the RGD-33. It weighed 420g, of which 200g was explosive. Range was about 35–50m depending on the arm of the thrower, and effective blast was 10m radius. *U.S. Army*

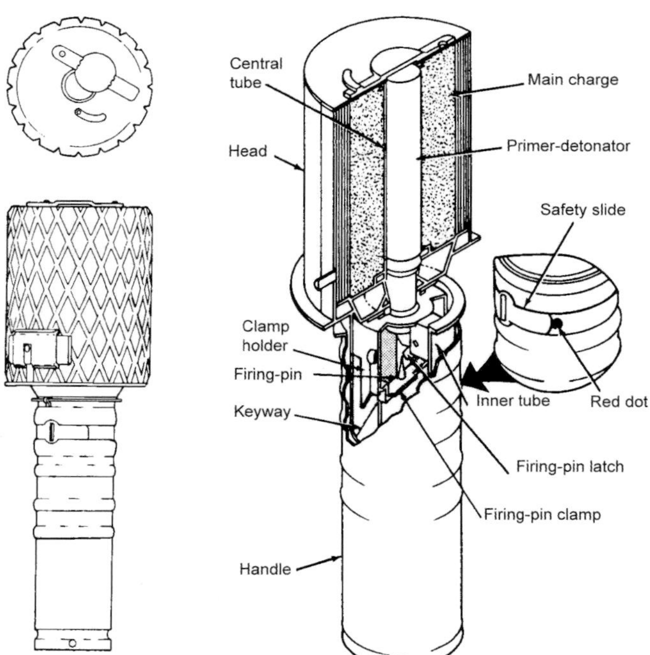

The RGD-33 grenades had an optional fragmentation sleeve. It was complicated to use—the fuse, handle, and warhead with fragmentation sleeve were stored separately and had to be combined. This is one reason why it was eventually replaced by the simpler RG-42. Both models had 4–5-second fuses. Weight was 750g with the fragmentation sleeve that also improved the kill radius from 10m to 15m. *U.S. Army*

Medium mortar teams had a lot of heavy equipment to carry. Usually there were four components: the tube, which was 1.22m (4ft) long and weighed 18.5kg, the baseplate (19.4kg), bipod (18.1kg), and ammunition (3.1kg–3.2kg). The crew of five included ammunition carriers. Abram Kotlyar: "In one of the battles, one of my soldiers was injured. Three people operate the mortar: the gun layer who aims the mortar, the firer, and during movement, the one who carried the mortar barrel. The firer carried the carriage that supports the mortar. The third soldier carried the baseplate that the mortar leaned on. And two other people carried the ammunition in boxes. So my third guy was injured, the one who carried the baseplate. But we had to move forward, and there were no replacements. I took the baseplate and continued to move forward. When the mortar fire started, everyone hit the ground. I'm on the ground and I felt the shelling debris hitting the baseplate I was carrying. It was steel, and it saved my life. If it wouldn't be for it, this fragment would have hit me. It was a pain to carry the baseplate, but it saved my life." *(BA) Fortepan/Vörös Hadsereg*

Below right: Soviet 82mm mortar development started with recalibrating the 81mm Stokes-Brandt mortar to 82mm (82-BM 36 where BM = *batalyonny minomyot* = battalion mortar). Soon, however, the Soviets developed their own, the 82-BM 37, which had a circular (rather than oblong) baseplate and recoil springs between barrel and bipod. Weight was also reduced, and this model remained in service throughout the war. Next came the 82-BM 41, which incorporated wheels to make it more mobile. A great idea, it wasn't successful until modified to produce the 82-BM 43, which did the business and became the standard Russian medium mortar of the war. Here, an 82-BM 37 mortar is prepared during the battle of Khalkhin Gol, Zhukhov's defeat of the Japanese in summer 1939. Note the combat box used to carry the ammunition: made of stamped sheet metal, it had a hinged lid, fingertip pressure catches, and carrying handles. *Albumwar2.com*

Left: The 50mm M38 (RM-38) mortar was based on the British Stokes of World War I and was man-portable, simple to set up, and a reliable source of indirect fire. Introduced in 1938, it was developed into the M-39 and, subsequently, the M-40. A new design, the M-41, took over and was produced until 1943, when it was decided that 50mm was too small a caliber to be effective. *U.S. Army*

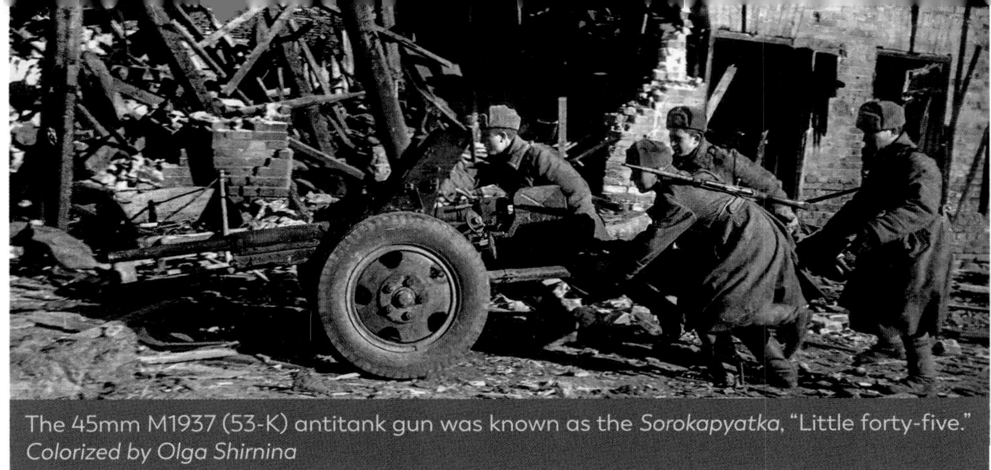
The 45mm M1937 (53-K) antitank gun was known as the *Sorokapyatka*, "Little forty-five." *Colorized by Olga Shirnina*

45mm M-42 antitank gun about to fire for a propaganda photo. This gun is the upgraded version of the M-37 with an extended barrel, strengthened breechblock, and wire wheels. These were eventually replaced by the disc type. The white canvas bag on the right-hand trail probably holds range poles. The box at the right is for the sights. Note the smoke pots. *Colorized by Olga Shirnina*

The ZIS-2 57mm antitank gun was designed in 1940 and entered service in 1941. Its cost and problems with ammunition saw the production line halted. In 1943, manufacture was restarted when it became obvious that the cheaper 45mm antitank guns couldn't penetrate the armor of new German tanks. In total, 10,000 ZIS-2s were built. *Fortepan/ Vörös Hadsereg*

The 76mm M1939 F-22 USV crew-served (5–7 men) divisional battery gun was designed by Vasiliy Grabin and introduced in 1939. The prewar USV gave way to the wartime F-22 and F-22 USV, and a total of 9,812 of all variants were produced during 1939–41. The Germans captured many and it was designated 7.62cm F.K.297(r). Rate of fire was 15rpm (max. range of 13.29km/8.26 miles). The photo shows the pneumatic road/cross-country tires of the M39 and the spoked wheel for horse-drawn guns or limbers. *RIA Novosti archive, image #716031 /Victor Kinelovskiy/WikiCommons (CC-BY-SA 3.0)*

The ZIS-3 76mm divisional gun model 1942 was an improved but simplified version of the F-22 USV, with upgraded barrel, suspension, tubular split trail, and muzzle brake. Crew of four comprised commander, gunner, loader, ammo carrier, although if other men were available they would put pressure on the trails when firing and help feed rounds to the loader. 48,500 artillery pieces were produced in total; 500 of the guns were mounted on tanks. While its primary purpose was against personnel and enemy artillery, increasingly it became the Red Army's main antitank gun because of the lack of ZiS-2s. It was ineffective against the German heavy tanks front-on or at long range, which forced the Soviet antitank units to use close-range ambush tactics. Its relative lightness—1,116kg (2,460lb) in combat—meant it could be maneuvered on the battlefield by hand, a definite plus. *Colorized by Olga Shirnina*

The 122mm howitzer M1938 (M-30) was usually towed by horse. Designed by Motovilikha Plants 92 and 9 design team and introduced in 1939, about 17,500 were produced to 1945. Its eight-man crew fired 122×284mm rounds at 5–6rpm to an effective range of 11.8km. This photo shows four M-30s on a direct fire mission in an urban setting. Note the lack of muzzle brake—a deliberate design decision; also the wedged log to reduce recoil. *Alexander Dmitriev/albumwar2.com*

Transport and Services

The major logistical weaknesses of the Red Army were shown up in the fighting against Poland and then the Winter War with the Finns. The supply and transport services were subsequently overwhelmed by Barbarossa. Fortunately, they had at hand two men who could solve the problems: the architect of the plan, former chief quartermaster of the Tsarist Russian Army, Konstantin Efimovich Goretskii, and General Andrei Vasilyevich Khrulev, who went on to become deputy chief of People's Commissar of Defense of the USSR and Head of Main Directorate of the Rear Services of the Red Army from 1941.

In 1942–1943 Khrulev also served as People's Commissariat for Railways. He did such a good job that he was buried on the Kremlin Wall necropolis and had the Military Academy of Logistical Support named after him. Goretskii and Khrulev put together a scheme for a centralized logistics structure for the Red Army that was approved by Stalin. On August 1, 1941, Khrulev took charge of the Main Directorate of the Rear of the Red Army (Glavnogo Upravleniia Tyla Krasnoi Armii), handling supply, transport, and medical care. The directorate's success was helped by its monopoly of transport through the Central Directorate of Military Communications—and this was made even easier on March 25, 1942, when Khrulev became Narkom (People's Commissar) of the People's Commissariat of Railways (NKPS). The Soviet concept of supply was, as Davie puts it,

A Lend-Lease jeep, one of over 400,000 trucks and jeeps included in a $11 billion package of materiel delivered by the United States, on the road towards Kustrin, a city on the Oder and the border with Germany. The photo shows a ZIS-5 towing a trailer, an ISU-152 tank destroyer in the background and horses and carts to the left. The sign in the foreground is the abbreviation for *kontrol'no-pasportnyy punkt* = checkpoint. *Waralbum.ru*

> radically different from the German/European model of "demand from below," where Divisional staffs sent requisitions up to Army supply officers to refill to standard levels, which resulted in all divisions being supplied more or less equally, while in the Red Army that only applied to the supply of rations and fodder. All combat supplies used a "central dispatch" model that allowed them to be sent to active Fronts and to starve inactive ones, while within the front the same process saw active Armies supplied first and within the Army directed to units that were successful in combat. The effect of this policy was to concentrate limited supplies at the point of decision and for the Center to determine where its greatest effort would be made.

The Directorate of the Rear controlled all transport other than air transport, and all supplies except weapons, ammunition, and technical equipment. It supervised medical and veterinary services, road maintenance, and other service agencies, while the supply of weapons and ammunition from factories to front-line units down to rifle regiments was in the hands of the Chief of Artillery.

The size of the Soviet Union meant that railways played a key role in getting supplies to the Red Army. Coordination of rail transport with military requirements was enabled early in the war as the NKPS was militarized early. When Barbarossa began to encroach on key areas, the Soviets were clued up enough to save much of their rolling stock and locomotives from the Germans. They had enough stock to move industries away from the battlefields, and were able to construct or maintain the lines necessary to supply their armies. Rail transport played a key role in attack as well as defense, usually extending only to army railheads, although it wasn't unknown for railheads to be established in the rear areas of rifle divisions.

Nevertheless, there were critical shortages of specialized rolling stock and of capacity on the rail lines, which meant that supply one way and evacuation the other of personnel and materiel had to be carefully managed. Delivery of ammunition and fuel always took precedence over other supplies. The Soviets also became adept—as the Germans were—in making the most of local resources and any Axis equipment they captured. Fuel supplies were always difficult as military pipelines were virtually non-existent.

For the infantryman at the front, the division was the key point in the supply chain as it had its own supply dump. The rear services at division level included the following groups:

- Organization and planning.
- Rations and fodder (including bakery).
- Intendance (clothing depot, artisans, and laundries).
- Fuel and lubricants.
- Motor transport which has one motor transport company.
- Technical equipment and supplies.
- Finance (office of the State Bank attached).
- Division Medical Officer (controls motor ambulances, medical battalions, collecting stations, divisional medical stations, pharmacy, and a delousing station).
- Division Veterinary Officer (controls a veterinary hospital, pharmacy, and motor vehicles to transport horses).
- Artillery supply group (controls weapons, equipment, and ammunition depot, an armory and a workshop).

Basic Supplies Carried by a Rifle Division

Supply	*Total units carried*	*With man, horse, gun, and machine*	*Carried by Bn or Bty train*	*Carried by Regt train*	*Carried by Div transport*
Rifle Division:					
Ammunition*	1.5	0.5	0.25	0.25	0.5
Fuel (refills)	2.0	1	–	0.5	0.5
Food (rations)	5	1	1 (in kitchens)	1	2
Grain feed (rations)	4	1–3[1]	–	2[1]	1
Bulk feed (rations)	4	1–2–3[2]	–	2–1[3]	1
GHQ Units:					
Ammunition*	1.5	0.5	0.5	–	In artillery train 0.5
Fuel (refills)	2	1	0.5	0.5	
Food (rations)	4	1	1	2	
*Units of fire					

[1] For mounts, artillery, and other draft animals—1 ration; for remainder—3 rations (after hauling). In the regiment's supply column—2 rations for mounts, artillery, and other draft animals.

[2] For mounts, artillery, and other draft animals—1 ration; for MG cart teams, medical, signal, and field kitchen animals—2 rations; for remainder—3 rations (after hauling).

[3] For mounts, artillery, and other draft animals—2 rations. For MG cart teams, medical, signal, and field kitchen animals—1 ration.

The divisional commander decided where supply points were established—usually near the boundary between division and regimental rear areas. They included an artillery dump, an ordnance workshop, a chemical equipment dump, a fuel dump, ration and fodder dumps, an assembly point for damaged vehicles, a clothing dump with a reserve of underwear and an intendance repair shop, and an assembly point for captured materiel.

To support an attack, divisional supply points were placed 6–7 miles from the front line. During an advance, that could become 12–18 miles behind the front line without the flow of supplies being impeded, although artillery supply units tended to be moved forward to within 2.5–3.5 miles of the battle front. The divisional Chief of Artillery Supply usually could be found with this advance unit. Advance mobile supply units with ammunition and food followed the troops in 6–9-mile bounds, using about 25 percent of all the division's motor vehicles.

Each division was usually provided with five rations of food and fodder, two refills of fuel, and 1.5 units of fire for all subordinate and attached units. The commander of a rifle regiment had a deputy for supply, who controlled:

- Rations and fodder (with ration dumps).
- Intendance.
- Technical equipment and supplies.
- Horse-drawn transport company.
- Finance officer (with State Bank agent).
- Regimental medical officer.
- Regimental veterinary officer.

The Chief of Artillery provided the rifle regiment with arms and ammunition from the artillery dump through the Chief of Artillery Supply. Supply transportation was requisitioned from the regimental commander's deputy for supply. Regimental ammunition dumps were located in the regimental rear area, 3–6 miles from the front line.

Rations and fodder supply units remained near the rear boundary of the regimental rear area. When a regiment was extended in mountain operations, regimental ammunition dumps were usually not deployed. Ammunition was delivered directly to battalion dumps by division transportation. When companies became extended, the battalion ammunition supply section was divided among the companies and company ammunition dumps were serviced by regimental transportation.

All this is good theory and by the end of the war supplies and logistics had improved considerably. However, for much of the war this wasn't the case: for example, on July 20, 1942, a report from 284th Rifle Division talked of its strength having been reduced to 3,172, and while over 3,000 replacements were in the process of arriving, there were only around 2,000 rifles/semiautomatic rifles and 200 PPSh SMGs. Lack of HE ammunition meant that artillery had to use armor-piercing in an antipersonnel role.

Boris Ginzburg was a political deputy in the Reserve Battalion, 232nd Independent Machine Gun–Artillery Battalion, in the 117th Fortified Position of the Southwestern Front in 1942. It was a well-built defensive position, but unfortunately supplies were lacking:

> July 3: On the whole, ammunition is a hot-button issue. Artillerymen have 24 shells for 4 guns, antitank riflemen don't have a single cartridge, there are not enough shells nor cartridges, there isn't a single submachine gun in the company, no SVTs, and on average there is one rifle for three people. I promise all of this to the guys, the commissar and the commander promise me, and the battalion commander promises them, and someone else makes the promise to the battalion commander, but things haven't budged an inch.

Ginzburg noted an improvement the next day but from an unexpected source:

> We received new armaments today … there was a great number of army privates going east through the fields and through our positions in disarray. Many were walking with weapons, and I decided to take these from them. Many of them did not give up the guns, but there were some that happily unloaded their "extra"—according to them—weight. I had to give some of them receipts … In this manner we were able to get nearly enough rifles, the antitank riflemen procured around 10 cartridges for the whole platoon, and Palkin procured an SVT. (*BA*)

Ammunition supplies took some time to improve after the problems caused by the speed of the German initial attacks. Both sides made great use of captured weapons and ammunition. *www.stavka.photos*

Rifle Division Transport

The organization of the rifle division went through various changes from June 1941 to December 1942 when it was set up by *Shtat* 04/550 (Shtat—*Shtatnoe raspisanie*—primarily denotes manpower, but its secondary meaning is as a synonym for TO&E) with 9,435 men in three rifle regiments, each of three battalions with transport provided by 1,719 horses, 437 wagons, 268 carts, 125 motor trucks, 15 tractors, and 4 passenger cars. Most of the motor vehicles were concentrated in:

- Rifle Regts (each): 1 GAZ-AA, 7 ZIS-5s (for the 120mm mortars)
- Artillery Regt: 1 GAZ-Type A workshop, 4 ZIS-5s, 15 STZ-5 tractors to pull the medium howitzers
- Transport Co: 2 GAZ-AAs, 45 ZIS-5s
- Medical Bn: 10 GAZ ambulances, 3 ZIS-5s for rations and 2 field kitchen trailers
- Chemical Defense Co: 6 GAZ-AA chemical trucks
- AT Gun Bn: 5 GAZ-AAs (munitions, fuel and rations), 12 ZIS-5s to pull the guns.

The corresponding Guards division had more men and weapons but the same vehicle allocation.

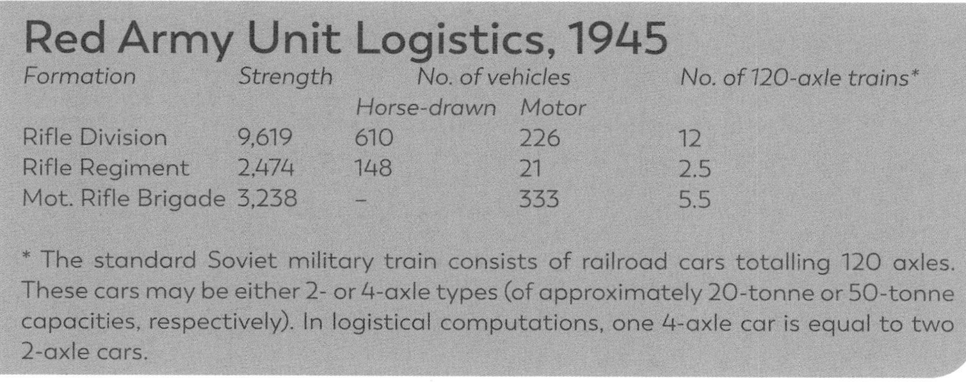

Red Army Unit Logistics, 1945

Formation	*Strength*	*No. of vehicles*		*No. of 120-axle trains**
		Horse-drawn	*Motor*	
Rifle Division	9,619	610	226	12
Rifle Regiment	2,474	148	21	2.5
Mot. Rifle Brigade	3,238	–	333	5.5

* The standard Soviet military train consists of railroad cars totalling 120 axles. These cars may be either 2- or 4-axle types (of approximately 20-tonne or 50-tonne capacities, respectively). In logistical computations, one 4-axle car is equal to two 2-axle cars.

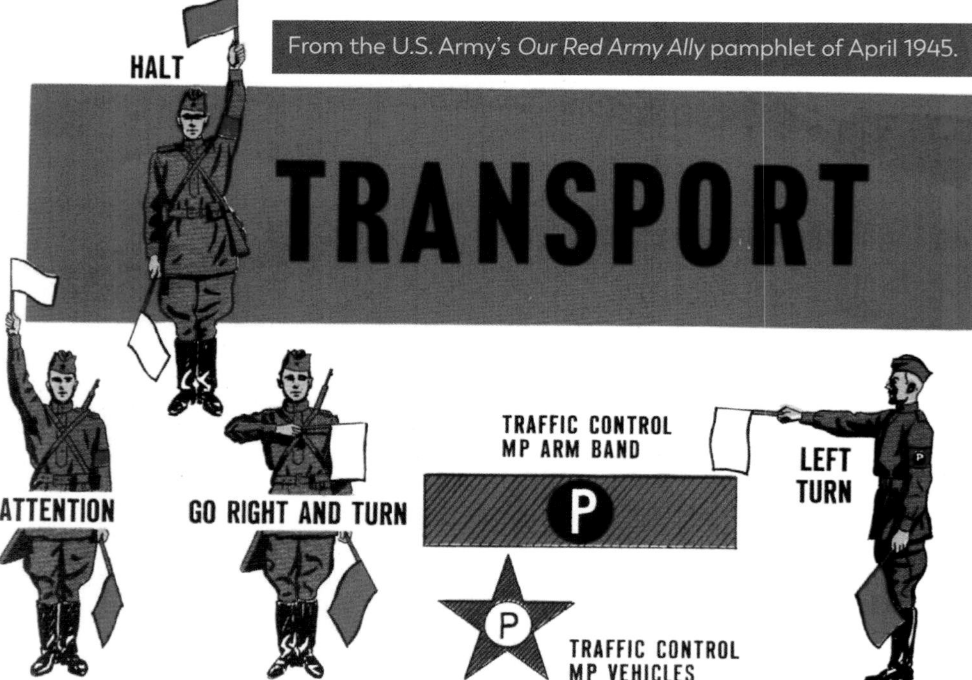

From the U.S. Army's *Our Red Army Ally* pamphlet of April 1945.

1. The 3-ton 4x2 Cargo (Ural-ZIS-5V) was produced in the Ural Factory of ZIS (*Zavod Imeni Stalina*; named after him from 1933 on). The ZIS-5 was a true workhorse for the Red Army. Because of the Soviet Union's lack of steel, the ZIS-5V had wooden elements, including the cab and the angular front bumper. The average numbers of trucks required to move Red Army units were:

Unit	*No. of trucks*	
	ZiS-S	*GAZ-AA*
Rifle Bn	100	
Artillery Bn	180	250
Rifle Regt	550	700
Regt howitzer bty	120	

2. The *rasputitsa* (muddy period after the rains) affected both sides. Here, Red Army soldiers, including women, push a ZiS-5 military truck which is stuck in the mud. Khatyan Dvoskin remembers: "To be on the offensive is challenging: we had great difficulties with food and ammo provision, vehicles got stuck in the mud, so we had to haul the trucks and the guns. It was especially trying in Ukraine. ... We particularly struggled with GAZ 2-A trucks with one drive axle. They got stuck for no reason. When American Studebakers arrived, whose three-drive axles allowed them to go anywhere, that was a different war. We moved forward and never had to heave a truck again, which was great relief." *(BA) Ivan Shagin via albumwar2.com*

3. A Lend-Lease International (Harvester) M-5-6x4 318 truck, one of around 3,000 sent to the Soviet Union. 500 6x6s were also sent. The M means military, the 5 shows a 5,000lb payload and the 318 denotes the 111-bhp 318-cid FBC-318B engine. They had Budd all-steel cargo bodies. *Online Photo Library of Romanian Communism Fotografia #C073*

4. A Soviet motorized unit drives through Bucharest in 1944. The motorcycle is an M-72 which was based on a BMW design for licensed production from 1939. *Waralbum.ru*

Rifle divisions carried 186 tonnes of munitions, 26.1 tonnes food, 11.7 tonnes fodder (2.9 tonnes grain and 6.8 tonnes hay), 9.9 tonnes fuel, all of which totals 233.7 tonnes, of which the motor transport company could carry 129 tonnes. Everything else—typically two-thirds of the whole load, including soldiers' baggage—was horse-drawn or carried by soldiers.

Supply installations servicing a unit were located in the unit's rear area: for a regiment, that extended to a depth of 5–7 miles; 18–22 for a division; and army rear areas extended to 95–125 miles, and fronts to 185–250 miles. Service organizations of rifle units and formations were usually established in rear of the combat line as shown in the diagram below.

Organization	*Distance from combat line (miles)*
Regimental ammunition dumps and artillery workshops	3–6
Regimental artillery supply dumps	3–6
Regimental medical stations	1.5–3
Regimental train, second echelon (incl. rations and fodder supply unit, transportation company equipment, veterinary aid station, and intendance workshop)	5–7.5
Division supply point	6–9.5
Division medical station	3.5–6
Field bakery and division veterinary hospital	One day's march
Division artillery supply installations	In regimental rear area near boundary of division rear area

Organization of rear services and supply channels of Red Army regiments, divisions, armies, and fronts. *U.S. Army*

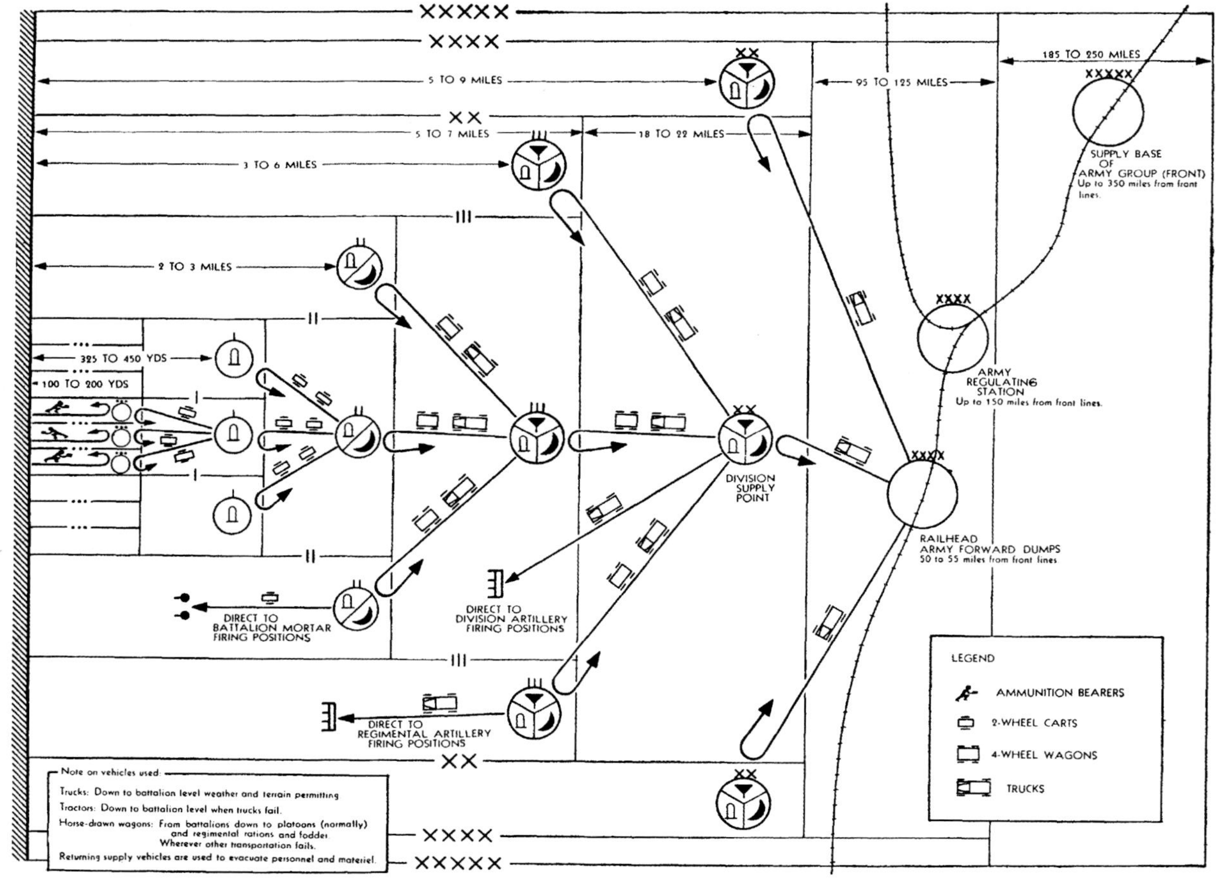

Size of the Red Army Transport Fleet

	Army	Stavka reserve	Military districts	Total
December 1941				
Motor vehicles (total)	197,678	3,420	110,457	311,555
Of which trucks	152,383	2,977	79,802	235,162
Tractors	17,217	359	18,710	36,286
Horses	608,817	162,549	516,275	1,287,641
November 1942				
Motor vehicles (total)	263,714	7,095	106,629	377,438
Of which trucks	195,618	5,677	72,461	273,776
Tractors	21,107	250	15,165	36,522
Horses	781,759	18,238	249,436	1,049,433
January 1945				
Motor vehicles (total)	366,959	20,362	145,279	532,600
Of which trucks	268,428	14,423	96,493	379,344
Tractors	40,139	1,730	14,203	56,072
Horses	791,611	29,303	233,240	1,054,154

As can be seen, the number of motor vehicles doubled during the war, and horse numbers dropped from summer 1942 to January 1944 because of heavy losses, the field army numbers being maintained by replacing them from the Stavka reserve and military districts. While truck numbers increased during the war, they hardly kept pace with increased workloads and horses still provided half the transport lift for the Red Army. Nevertheless, by use of railways along with trucks and horses, the Red Army managed to sustain its great advances of 1944 and 1945.

There were two echelons of regimental and division services. The first echelon of regimental services included ammunition supply and medical installations. The second echelon included transport for rations, fodder, fuel and other supplies, a veterinary aid station, and a quartermaster workshop. The first echelon of division services was the division supply point.

The second echelon included a field bakery and a veterinary hospital. Usually, the division medical station was in a regimental rear area along the axis of advance. This pattern for the organization of rear areas varied according to the dictates of operational requirements, terrain, weather conditions, and available transportation.

Polish First Army trucks await the signal to move out. The Soviets supplied equipment—often Lend-Lease—to the armies of countries that fought under the Red Army's flag. *NAC*

Horses

Mongolia was the major supplier of horses for the Soviets. In 1940 the country had over 20 million, but 11 million of these were lost to the advancing Germans in 1941. They were used extensively both for logistics but also as cavalry mounts. The Red Army used 3.5 million horses but were always short—a 1941 rifle division identified 3,039 horses on strength, but this was reduced during the war to 1,196—partly as the manpower levels were reduced by design, partly because of attrition. Rifle regiments used horses for supply, with horse-drawn wagons performing most tasks. Transport companies had 21 each: 12 for rations/fodder, six for QM supplies such as clothing, and three for HQ. Of course, there were other benefits to working with horses, as Abram Sapozhnikov remembered:

> We were driving two carts with equipment, when two planes appeared in the distance. Suddenly a soldier shouts to me, "Comrade lieutenant, the planes are upon us." I looked up and saw the Messerschmitts with swastikas. I only managed to cry out, "Run and lie face down." The carts remained standing on the road. Each aircraft shot two rounds from large-caliber machine guns. One horse, the best in our battalion, was killed, another horse was injured, and one soldier was lightly wounded. The rest survived. Everything went quiet then. I found our telephone line, turned it on. My future wife was on duty … I reported that I could not move ahead, for one of our horses had been killed, and we could not manage the equipment and telephone connection by ourselves. I was instructed to get off the road and wait for reinforcements. Naturally, we dragged the dead horse with us, skinned it and had a nice meal. When I received a new horse, I proceeded with the mission. (*BA*)

Sled horses being fed with woven straw German overboots as Soviet soldiers pick up abandoned German uniforms. Thick, felt guard boots with wooden soles were supplied to those in the Wehrmacht as winter clothing. However, shortfalls in uniform forced the German servicemen to make an ersatz version of such shoes from straw harnesses. *Natalia Bode/Sovetskaya Rossiya*

A good example of the logistical use of horses in the Red Army, as horse-drawn light and heavy artillery move through the streets of Budapest. *Fortepan/Vörös Hadsereg*

Dog sleds have always been important in the north—in this case to pull *akjas* loaded with ammunition from an underground cache. *Colorized by Olga Shirnina*

The German Shepherd was the favored dog for military service and in the early years tended to be already trained—such as police and hunting dogs. Training schools were established in the 1930s and produced dogs for rescue, communication, transporting supplies—First Aid, for example—pulling sleds and small carts, security, tracking people and mines, attack and, controversial in some quarters even then, antitank dogs. This photo shows a German Shepherd with handler in Budapest. *Fortepan/Vörös Hadsereg*

Communications

The Red Army 1942 *Infantry Manual* states: "Control in combat is achieved through continuous communications attained by use of various means (radio, telephone, motorcycles, bicycle, light and sound signals, liaison officers, foot and mounted messengers)." Radios in particular were in big demand but there were shortages. These were alleviated by equipment from Great Britain and under Lend-Lease from the United States, the latter supplying nearly 400,000 field telephones, nearly a million miles of field telephone wire, and more than 40,000 radio sets. By the end of the war at least 30 percent of Red Army signal equipment was of standard American and British materiel. The organic allotment of radios in a Soviet rifle division was significantly less than the Western Allies, just over 10 percent of a U.S. infantry division, but radio was used as an auxiliary to wire, principally in command and artillery fire control nets. In special situations large quantities of additional radio equipment could be furnished from higher-echelon signal reserves. For example, 27,174 radios were used in the Belorussian operation in June–July 1944. Boris Tsalik trained and served as a radio officer:

> I was an officer and I had a few radio stations. So I used to go to the front line with a radio station, even in front of the infantry, because the infantry was located, for example, in the forest, but we needed an unobstructed space to avoid the radio noise. This is why we were on the front line of military action. My radio stations helped me identify more than forty enemy airplanes that were destroyed. …
>
> First of all, a radio station must be functional. If it stopped working then there won't be any connection. If there were any serious malfunctions I sat down at the radio station and worked myself. I had first grade skills in working with a telegraph key, so I could work with telegraph. In the second part of the war, when the Red Army was finishing up in Ukraine, I was transferred to Moscow to learn how to work with American radio stations. … The difference with the Soviet radio stations was that American stations were more reliable, their coverage range was bigger and they had better amplifiers. It was possible to just bring the microphone into a tent without inviting the head officers into the radio station's booth. Such an amplifier was quite effective. And the engine was good, too. … A Willys engine was installed in those radio stations and it worked off a starter. That is, those stations were a sensation in communications during the war. I had to provide connection: the communicator has to speak to the recipient of that communication. I had to provide clear sound for the recipient. If the microphone didn't have clear reception, then I had to use the telegraph key to receive a message. (*BA*)

Communications in the Red Army was mainly based on wire. The rifle regiment's signal company had 50 men divided into 2 x telephone and telegraph (T&T) platoons and 1 x radio platoon. The first T&T platoon had three squads to establish wire communications with the battalions; the second established wire communications within the command, staff, and rear areas of the regiment, and maintained the message center. The radio platoon established and operated the regiment's radio nets.

The rifle division's signal battalion had 130 men: an HQ, 1 x signal communications company, 1 x signal construction company, 1 x maintenance and repair platoon, and 1 x supply section.

Corps had an independent signal battalion of 250 men: HQ company, 1 x telephone company (3 x platoons each with 3 trucks, 9 telephones, and 15 miles of field cable), 1 x radio

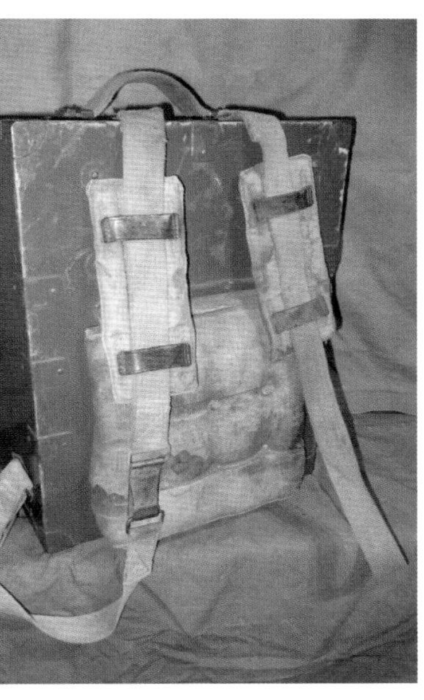

The man-portable A-7 (plus its variations) VHF transceiver with frequency modulation was used for communication in rifle brigades and regiments. While signal flags were often used during the early stages, as the war progressed experience showed that radio was the main and sometimes only means of providing command and control of troops. Soviet communications equipment was materially helped by British and American supplies. The United States, alone, provided nearly 400,000 field telephones, nearly a million miles of field telephone wire, and more than 40,000 radio sets. It is believed that in October 1945, at least 30 percent of Red Army signal equipment consisted of standard American and British materiel. *John Gibbon*

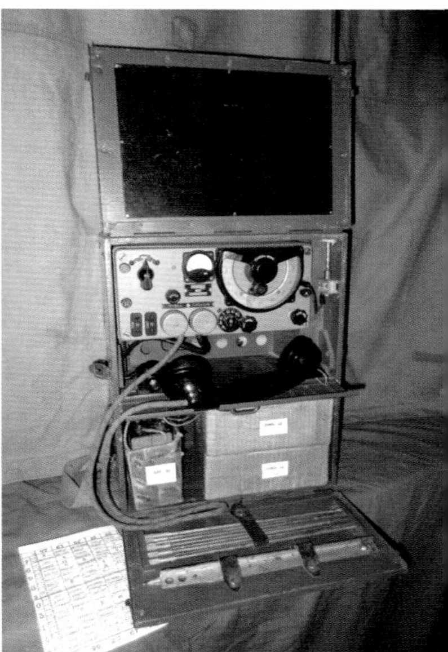

Training was definitely "on the job" for many in communications. Khatyan Dvoskin remembers: "I had to familiarize myself with the equipment, for I had never dealt with radio, I hadn't even had time to pass first-year exams at the polytechnic. And so, I read while we traveled. The chief shouts, 'I need connection.' I was ready to carve my heart out and stick it in that radio. I opened the set, pulled the receiver-transmitter out, saw that six lamps were on and one was out. For the rest of my life, I will remember the name of that lamp, SB242, special barium lamp. All others were 2K, 2M, and this one was SB242. I had a spare set. When I took it out and inserted a new one, the noise reappeared, making me the happiest man alive." (*BA*) The RBM-1 field radio (seen here) was an amplitude-modulated transmitter for voice or CW operation. With a 1.8m (6ft) antenna, it had a range of 10 miles subject to weather conditions. Weight with battery was 17.23kg (38lb). Senior Sergeant Khatyan Dvoskin on the left is tuning or calibrating and the junior sergeant on the right is receiving a message. Photo dated 1944. *Blavatnik Archive*

Busy Red Army signalers repairing, replacing, or putting up wire in Vienna. One carries one of the many variations of a cable reel. The photo also shows American Lend-Lease trucks with troops and towing artillery, and two M-72 motorcycle combinations, one with a jerrycan. The full utilization of captured signal equipment (especially wire for duplicating lines) was part of Soviet signal doctrine, and special reconnaissance groups were sent out on the personal initiative of the chief signal officers of regiments and higher units to collect usable equipment left by the enemy. *Yevgeny Khaldei/TASS Newsreel*

Soviet officers and NCOs confer over map coordinates by telephone. Khatyan Dvoskin: "During the first two years, there was hardly any radio communication. It came later: first there was the 12-RT radio, then more powerful RSB and RB radios." *(BA) World War photos*

A signaler taking notes. Khatyan Dvoskin: "I only had a slight wound ... but significant, in my jaw. It stopped working, I couldn't speak, which was disastrous ... So, I had to switch to telegraph key for a week, which was lucky, because the telegraph key tripled the communication range. That's why I switched to the key in our division." *(BA) World War photos*

Signaler receiving information from the Soviet Information Bureau (Sovinformburo), June 1942. Sovinformburo was formed two days after the war began and supervised the work of war correspondents, transmitting daily reports. Its broadcasting studio was in Sverdlovsk (now Yekaterinburg) between autumn 1941 and March 1943, when it was moved to Kuibyshev (now Samara). *RIA Novosti archive, image #87381/Loskutov/WikiCommons (CC-BY-SA 3.0)*

company, 1 x signal construction company (6 cable-laying trucks), 1 x technical maintenance and repair platoon, and 1 x supply section. The HQ company included a telephone platoon to set up and operate communications within the HQ, a messenger platoon, and an air liaison platoon. For extended operations the signal battalion was reinforced with one or more telephone companies.

An army's signal regiment had 700–800 men to establish communications for army HQ, staff, and rear area installations. For communications with subordinate units and formations, it received one additional telephone company for each corps. It consisted of HQ, 1 x T&T battalion (this included 1 x teletype and telephone exchange, 1 x radio company—1 x transmitter for each subordinate formation, 6 x semi-mobile transmitters, and 5 x radio trucks—and a messenger company with 50 men, 12 staff cars, and 6 motorcycles), 1 x signal construction battalion (2 x cable companies, each with 6 cable-laying trucks), 1 x signal intelligence company and 1 x service battalion (1 x transport company, 1 x maintenance company and 1 x supply platoon).

Communications were established down and to the left, and supporting units were responsible for communications with the supported units. Wire facilities were heavily reinforced for operations. For example, TM 30-430 mentions one offensive situation during which "150 command and observation posts were set up in one rifle division sector by the division and supporting artillery. Approximately 30 switchboards were used to connect some 700 circuits joining the various command observation posts."

Code

The Soviets were very aware of signals intelligence and had strict conventions when it came to communications. Conversations concerning operations could not be sent in the clear. Field orders and reports on decisions, from division and higher, were permitted to be transmitted by radio, in code, only if no other means of communication was possible. The importance of this was emphasized by the fact that violations could become the basis of a court martial for disclosing military secrets. Clear text by radio was permitted in artillery to direct fire, but in all clear text messages, unit numbers were referred to by codenames. However, it wasn't always successful as a German field commander commentated:

> I must point out that the Soviet command was not able to assign enough trained radio operators to the combat units … As a result, the radio operators at the front line used only simple codes and we were nearly always able to intercept and decode their radio messages without any difficulty. Thus we obtained quick information on the front situation, and frequently on Soviet intentions as well: sometimes I received such reports from our monitoring stations earlier than the situation reports of our own combat troops and was able to make my decisions accordingly.

Medical and Veterinary Services

As with other special services, these were kept to a minimum in field units. Specialized units were part of the technical services reserve and were organized into teams with ample personnel and equipment. So, medical teams in rifle battalions and regiments were kept to 5–7 men. Their aim was to administer first aid and evacuate wounded to the divisional level where a medical battalion was capable of emergency surgery, but whose main mission was sorting, dressing, and evacuating wounded. The medical battalion had a sorting unit, an ambulance platoon, a divisional aid station, a collecting company, and an epidemic control unit.

The main medical services for field units were concentrated at army level. The army's medical battalion was organized into surgical and hospital teams. It allotted reinforcing elements to the divisions and mobile corps. The number of such teams corresponded generally to the number of subordinate rifle corps, rifle divisions, and mobile corps. The surgical team had a surgeon, 3–5 physicians, 4–5 surgical nurses, 5–6 orderlies and a recorder who kept the administrative records and recorded each operation. The hospital team was organized into sections according to types of injury. Each section consisted of a surgeon, a physician, 2–3 surgical nurses, and 5–7 orderlies. The infectious diseases section of the hospital team consisted of a physician, a nurse, 3–4 orderlies, and an X-ray and physiotherapy unit.

Excellent Medic award. From the 1930s teaching nurses to cope with battle became a standard component of training. The fighting in Poland and the Soviet-Finnish War increased the impetus. In 1939 the All-Union Society of the Red Cross and Red Crescent USSR trained some 40,000 reserve nurses (only 9,000 nurses were trained 1933–38). After *Barbarossa* there was further expansion as evacuation hospitals had to be created. By December 31, 1941, the Red Cross and Red Crescent had had trained 216,809 nurses and 355,445 sanitary brigade members, swelling Red Army medical ranks to 200,000 doctors, 300,000 nurses, and 500,000 sanitary brigade members. The trouble was that there was a big jump between theory and practice. "Everything seems so nice and neat and orderly when you're learning, but when you are actually involved in treating wounded, your arms are covered with blood up to your elbows." (Grant, 2022) The nurses' dedication speaks for itself: 72% of injured and 91% of sick Red Army troops returned to the front. *Simon Vanlint*

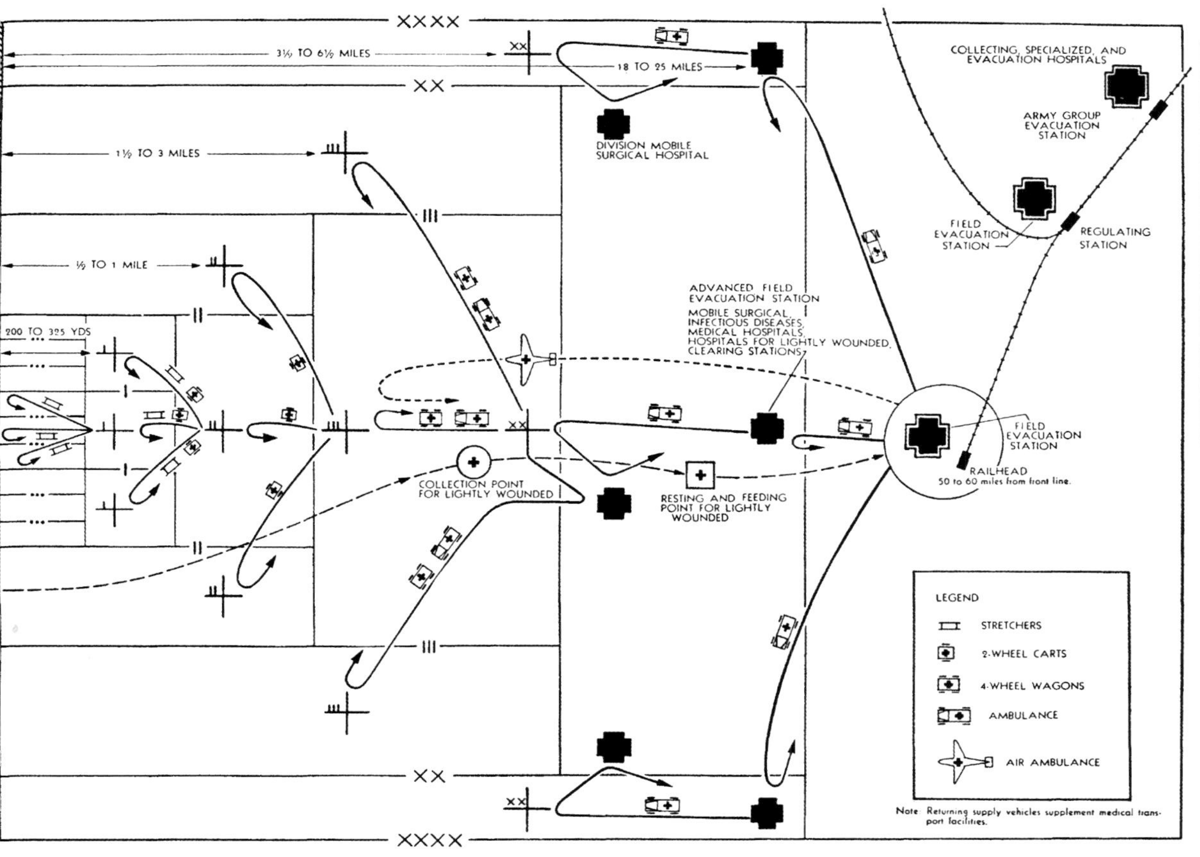

Diagram showing the process for moving casualties from the front line (at left). Note the NATO symbology of single stroke = company, double = battalion, triple = regiment, x = brigade, xx = division, xxxx = army. The casualty is evacuated to a holding area where he is transported by cart to a collection point and, if lightly wounded, onto a Mobile Surgical Hospital. The more seriously wounded are transported by ambulance to an Advanced Field Evacuation Station where they could be treated or evacuated. *U.S. Army*

The army convalescent battalion was capable of caring for 1,000 cases. It had four convalescent companies, a dental clinic, an infectious diseases ward, and a pharmacy. Each convalescent company had a dressing station manned by 2 physicians, 3 nurses, and 3–4 orderlies.

The veterinary units were organized similarly with organic veterinary units of horse-drawn field troops kept to a minimum. The veterinary aid station of a rifle division, with around 1,700 horses, had 11 men. As with the medical services, the main veterinary services were concentrated at the army level. Each army had two veterinary hospitals, each capable of caring for approximately 250 horses, and one or two veterinary evacuation hospitals. Leonid Ulitsky kept a wartime diary:

> On June 22 … at noon Molotov announced on the radio that the Germans had crossed the border and started the war against the Soviet Union without a declaration. Several days later I went to the military commissariat since I already submitted my application to enlist. They looked at my application, registered me right on the spot, and gave me a referral to the Kharkov Medical Military School. My military service started on July 3, 1941. Because of the war, it took us only six or seven months to finish a three-year school. However, we did not graduate in Kharkov. At first, when the Germans captured Kiev and were drawing close to Kharkov, we were transformed into a rifle regiment and sent to defend Kharkov. … Then suddenly it was announced, I don't remember the date,

that in accordance with the order of the Supreme Commander, all Kharkov schools—not just medical military schools, all schools—were to be evacuated to the east.

[We] went to Ashgabat, where we … resumed studying. Then we took our final exams, obtained the title "military medic," and went to Moscow to receive appointments to different fronts. … I received an appointment to go to the Kalinin Front … When I arrived at the 469th Rifle Regiment of the 250th Division, the total number of soldiers was no greater than 300–350, even though there had been over 10,000 before it joined the fighting. … When I came there and started to meet the team, I was very impressed to meet Maria Kalinovna Pavlenko, the commander of the stretcher-bearer platoon. There was always a platoon of stretcher bearers in a medical company of the regiment, to carry the injured first to a battalion aid station and then to a regiment aid station. After receiving first aid, the injured people were transported to a medical-sanitary battalion.

Anyhow, that Maria Kalinovna Pavlenko not only broke out of the [Smolensk] encirclement by herself—she was the platoon commander—but also evacuated ten carts with the injured. Her name was put forward for the title Hero of the Soviet Union, but medics rarely received this award in 1942 and 1943. It almost never happened, so she received the Order of Lenin instead. She was the only woman in our division who had the Order of Lenin.

Our regiment aid station received up to 600 wounded every three days … but had only two or three doctors and four aid workers. Imagine how hard we had to work to not only dress wounds and administer painkillers to everybody, but also perform blood transfusions in certain extreme cases. We had a shortage of doctors and medical aides for such an enormous, difficult job. …

When the regiment was advancing, we were only 200–300 meters away, behind the last, the third, battalion, in order to set up quickly and provide help. When a regiment was on the defensive, we were about two kilometers away from the front. That's how it was usually set up. During a march, we went in a column along with the regiment. If there were Germans ahead, the battalions went into the battle, and we moved back

Two orderlies carry a bandaged casualty from a large medical tent (*palatka*) with others linked to it. All wear felt overboots (*valenki*) which could be padded out—with straw or paper, for example—to keep the feet warm. Rubber galoshes could also be added but needed to be soaked in hot water so that they could be stretched to fit. Without these galoshes, boots would disintegrate in slush. *RIA Novosti archive, image #662767/Anatoliy Garanin/WikiCommons (CC-BY-SA 3.0)*

Field medics led a perilous existence. Here, a field medic is seen bandaging a wounded man during a battle. Many achieved great fame. Chief Petty Officer Yekaterina Illarionovna Mikhailova served with the 369th Separate Battalion of the Marine Corps of the Danube Military Flotilla. She was awarded the Order of Lenin, two Orders of the Red Banner, Orders of the Patriotic War of the 1st and 2nd degrees, medals, including the Medal for Courage and the Florence Nightingale Medal—and in May 1990 President Mikhail Gorbachev honoured her with the title Hero of the Soviet Union. *www.stavka.photos*

a little and set up the aid station. ... Here is how we set up our regimental aid station: we had an intake facility, a dressing room, and an evacuation department. We had such functional facilities for triaging the wounded and so on. The platoon of stretcher bearers went to the front to carry the wounded back. Then we also had dog-drawn sleds. There was one regiment with dog-drawn sleds in the army. The service of those dogs was invaluable. Each sled had one driver. Two sleds followed his lead. These sleds also evacuated the injured from the battlefield. (*BA*)

The Vets

It's all too easy to forget the veterinarian contribution to the Red Army. The number of horses in the army was considerable, not just for logistics but also because of its sizable cavalry units. This meant that—as with the human side—there was a steady stream of animals to be cared for. Any sick and wounded horses that could keep up with their units weren't evacuated, but those that needed to be were sent to advance veterinary aid stations established by the regimental veterinary hospitals on the line of evacuation nearest the main concentration of horses, normally near the regimental ammunition dump. The regimental veterinary hospitals were usually established in the regimental rear areas some 5 to 7 miles from the battle line. Those that needed to went on to divisional veterinary hospitals. From there, horses were evacuated to veterinary evacuation and field hospitals in army rear areas and to army group (front) veterinary hospital bases as necessary. *Colorized by Olga Shirnina*

Strategy and Tactics*

The Red Army's 1942 *Infantry Tactics Manual* acknowledges the importance of the infantry, which "accomplishes the hardest mission: annihilation of the enemy in close combat ... Infantry alone has the capacity of capturing and retaining territory. ... It can maneuver and conduct operations in any type of terrain, any climatic conditions, any time of day, any weather." It also "regards operations conducted by the infantry as those of combined arms and services with a wide participation of various combat techniques: artillery, tanks and aircraft."

The problems that arose in the debacle of 1941 informed the manual: "Retreat is permissible in exceptional cases. ... [It] must be orderly ... a temporary measure ... [it] cannot start without order of the superior commander no matter what the situation may be not even if full encirclement is threatening. ... Infantry must not fear encirclement. It must be able to come out of it in an organized fashion."

It introduces "new concepts"—the artillery and air offensives that would characterize Soviet assaults in later war—and talks about deep defenses with antitank, antiartillery, and antiaircraft capabilities. "Fortification measures must secure longevity and stability for defensive operations. Every inhabited locality and individual building must be turned into strongpoints, genuine forts with all-round defense assuring longevity even in the case they are encircled by the enemy."

Soviet infantry units had great strength in automatic weapons and mortars. Their moving weight was low, and while the rifle units had only horse transport, which could be slow, they could move across country and difficult terrains. Their supply capacity—as we have seen—was adequate for heavy combat, but their maintenance facilities were inadequate and had to be supplemented by army resources.

Soviet tactical employment of infantry was predicated on rapidity of maneuver of small groups, concentration of fire of automatic weapons, and shock action. In fluid situations, rapid deployment and immediate engagement were the rule. In more stable situations, engagement with the enemy was generally preceded by thorough reconnaissance and planning, and detailed rehearsals.

The basic building block of any army is the infantry squad. It eats, fights, and—all too often—dies together. *From the fonds of the RGAKFD in Krasnogorsk www.stavka.photos*

*This section makes heavy use of, and in places paraphrases, the U.S. Dept of Defense's *Handbook on USSR Military Forces*, Chap V Tactics, November 1, 1945.

War is energy sapping—long periods of fear and physical exertion take their toll. Here knackered infantryman grab a few minutes' rest. *From the fonds of the RGAKFD in Krasnogorsk www.stavka.photos*

The Rifle Regiment

The key to Red Army infantry tactics was the rifle regiment which generally attacked on a front 1,500 yards wide, an interior battalion on a front up to 700 yards, a company up to 350 yards, and a platoon up to 100 yards. On the defensive, a battalion occupied an area up to 2,000 yards wide and 1,500 to 2,000 yards deep, and a company occupied an area up to 700 yards wide and 700 yards deep. The rifle regiment had several specialized units and a significant contingent of automatic weapons.

1941 Rifle Regt	*1943 Rifle Regt*	*1944–45 Guards Rifle Regt*[1]
3 Rifle Battalions	3 Rifle Bns	3 Rifle Bns
1 Submachine gun Co[2]	1 SMG Co	2 SMG Cos (added in July)
1 Antitank Bty (4 x 45mm)[3]	1 Antitank Rifle Co[4]	3 Antitank Pls (ea 2 x 45mm)
1 Artillery Bty (4 x 76mm)	1 Antitank Bty (6 x 45mm)	2 Artillery Pls (ea 2 x 76mm)
1 Mortar Bty [5]	1 Artillery Bty (4 x 76mm)	1 Mortar Co (7 x 120mm)
	1 Mortar Bty (4 x 120mm)	

[1] The Guards rifle regiment had a similar configuration to the standard regiment but with two SMG companies and extra weapons in the battalions (where the ATR were sited). It was still horse-drawn (save for the 120mm mortar company).

[2] The SMG company was tasked with rapid flanking moves, infiltration, security of accompanying tanks and as a mobile reserve.

[3] The antitank gun battery, together with battalion antitank guns, was used to repel tank attacks in vulnerable sectors. Regimental and battalion antitank guns, together with the regimental artillery, were used extensively for direct fire in support of river crossings and assault of fortified positions.

[4] The ATR company provided antitank security in all phases of combat.

[5] The heavy mortar battery was used under centralized control during artillery preparation on the offensive and for laying down barrages on the defensive. It was under the control of supported units in the assault phase of the offense and decentralized defense.

On the March

A Red Army infantry regiment, acting as an advance guard of a division, was tasked with overcoming enemy outposts, occupying terrain for deployment of the division, and organizing preliminary reconnaissance. It advanced in the following order (see sketch overleaf): advance guard preceded by reconnaissance elements, the main body, the flank guards, and the rearguard. The advance guard was an infantry battalion reinforced by artillery and engineers. The main body had several sections, each comprising a balanced fighting group of approximately battalion size. The main body was flanked by security groups—rifle platoons reinforced with HMGs and ATRs. The rearguard was a reinforced rifle platoon. If the regiment advanced along an exposed flank, the flank guard on the exposed side was increased to approximately a battalion. Artillery elements which formed parts of the main body were always ready to support the advance guard. During long halts, artillery habitually deployed for action, while antitank units reconnoitred and deployed in sectors especially vulnerable to attack by tanks.

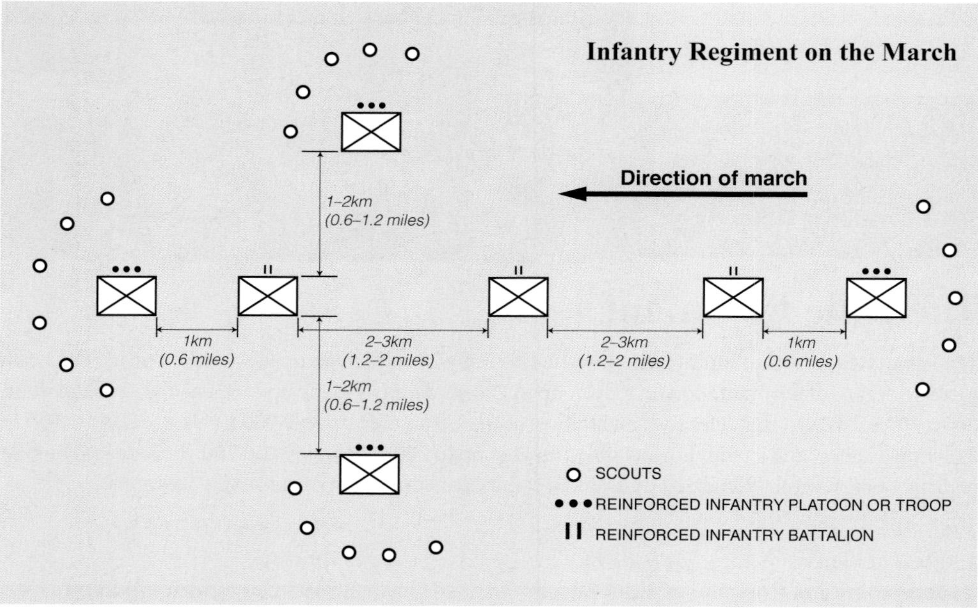

If the advance guard encountered only disorganized resistance, it overpowered enemy rearguards while the main body continued advancing. If the advance guard encountered organized resistance at a well-fortified position, the regiment deployed for action and tried to overpower the opposition by speed of maneuver and shock action. If the enemy was fully prepared to defend organized positions, the regiment secured advantageous ground for the deployment of the division and for organized intensive reconnaissance. During the advance the commander retained his command post in the advance guard.

In Attack

Infantry generally had two missions in attack: first, to break into the forward defense lines of the enemy and destroy or neutralize them; second, depending on the overall objective of the division, to overcome all enemy resistance in the assault sector including enemy artillery positions. Assaults were conducted in three distinct phases: preparation, execution of the initial mission, and penetration of the enemy defenses in depth in the execution of the subsequent missions.

The first mission was handled by assault groups: a typical one consisted of three to five engineers, a rifle platoon and several antitank rifles—although some battalion mortars and guns were assigned to the various assault groups according to the fire plans. HMGs were either allotted to the assault groups or retained under centralized control. According to the demands of the situation, regimental and, less frequently, divisional specialized arms were distributed among the assault groups.

If time permitted, the assault groups rehearsed the plan. These rehearsals were generally conducted both in daylight and at night over terrain like that of the contemplated operation and far enough removed from the enemy to escape his observation and interference.

It was considered imperative that the final artillery barrage was laid so that there was minimal time between it and the moment that the infantry reached the enemy's forward defense lines. Regimental and battalion antitank guns and mortars continued to fire on their targets until the last

Soviet Concept of the Coordinated Attack
Mission: To destroy enemy forces guarding the approaches to communication center X.
Forces available: Infantry division.
Enemy forces: Two infantry regiments and two artillery regiments.
Plan of maneuver: 1st Regt to advance to Objective A through breach made by the neighboring division. 2nd Regt, using the same breach, to advance to Obj B, leaving one battalion to deal with points of resistance C and D. 1st Bn, 3rd Regt to penetrate enemy defenses and join 2nd Regt at Obj C and provide flank security for 2nd Regt. 3rd Bn, 3rd Regt to penetrate enemy defenses and join 2nd Regt at Obj E. 2nd Bn, 3rd Regt to penetrate enemy defenses and join 1st Regt at Obj A. *U.S. Army*

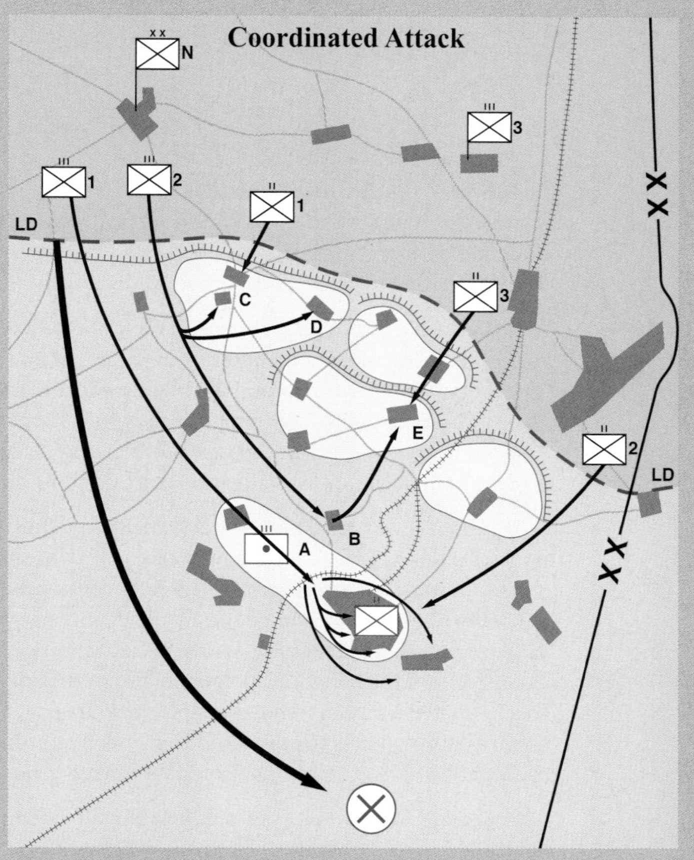

possible moment. The infantry had to be placed to reach the enemy forward lines a maximum of two minutes after the artillery barrage had lifted. During the assault, antitank guns and mortars reverted to the control of the supported units. Regimental artillery supported the assault in depth and prepared to displace forward. Battalion commanders did not commit their units in extended fire duels with the enemy centers of resistance; instead, they moved ahead, leaving small detachments to deal with the bypassed enemy.

When the infantry advance reached the enemy's artillery positions, it was down to the regimental reserve, assisted by some of the assault groups, to widen the breach, destroy bypassed centers of resistance, and exploit the breakthrough. The remainder of the assaulting force consolidated captured positions, prepared to repel counterattacks, or regrouped and continued the advance.

If tanks accompanied the infantry attack, regimental and battalion artillery concentrated fire on enemy antitank defenses. Infantry and engineers protected the tanks from hostile infantry, neutralized antitank minefields and other antitank obstacles, and helped evacuate damaged tanks. Tanks were not to outdistance their supporting infantry by more than 400 yards.

Pursuit

The slightest indication of the enemy's intention to withdraw from combat was a signal for every Soviet commander to initiate pursuit. Once started, the pursuit could only be halted by the senior commander. To stop the enemy withdrawing and forming march columns, infantry battalions increased pressure along the entire sector and the artillery and mortar batteries conducted interdictory fire on road junctions and assembly areas. The commander moved his reserves forward, grouped them into reinforced platoons, and deployed them for rapid advance in the direction of the main effort. The SMG company, grouped by platoons, infiltrated the enemy's rear area, disrupting his lines of communication and control.

As the pursuit developed, artillery and mortars advanced by bounds so that one echelon was ready for fire missions on request from the pursuing elements, while the other echelon displaced. The antitank rifle company and the regimental antitank battery organized protection of the flanks against counterattacks. Rear-area security groups kept the lines of supply clear of enemy stragglers. The engineer officer organized obstacle-clearing detachments which marched with the pursuing elements and facilitated the advance of artillery, mortars, tanks, and supply vehicles.

If motorized transport were available, pursuit detachments were organized and sent in parallel columns along secondary roads to overtake the enemy and strike him from the flanks and rear. A motorized pursuit group generally consisted of a rifle company, a reconnaissance squad, a machine-gun platoon, an engineer squad, and an antitank-gun team. If possible, each pursuing vehicle was provided with an AAMG. If tanks were available for the pursuit, infantry riders were assigned from the battalions. Regimental mortars advanced with the infantry, but if halftracks or other suitable transport were available, mortars could be loaned to tank units for exploitation of the breakthrough. As the pursuing elements outdistanced the original battalion assault teams, so the latter teams were also organized into pursuit groups.

During the pursuit, the regimental staff organized flank and rear security detachments, controlled the operations of the reconnaissance elements, organized coordination between the pursuing groups and their supporting units, and provided for continuous supply of ammunition and fuel.

In Defense

The objectives stated in Red Army defensive doctrine were to hold important positions with small forces; to utilize natural and artificial obstacles; to inflict heavy losses on the enemy by an organized fire of all weapons, thus forcing him to abandon the attack; and finally, to destroy him by a determined counterattack. Red Army doctrine for the organization of defensive positions prescribes the following requirements:

- The positions should be established in depth.
- Each defensive area and its parts should be capable of all-around defense.
- The defense should be supported by planned counterattacks.
- The fire plan should be designed to provide fire trap concentration on sectors subject to probable enemy attack.

In setting up defensive positions, all commanders were responsible for the construction of field fortifications, shelters, main and reserve command and observation posts, and main, alternate, and night-firing positions for artillery and mortars. All defense installations and fields of fire were checked by the commander and the chief of engineers. In the Red Army, lack of care and thoroughness in organizing and executing the construction of defense installations was considered one of the most serious of military offenses.

Tactical doctrines of the Red Army defined two types of defense: centralized and decentralized.

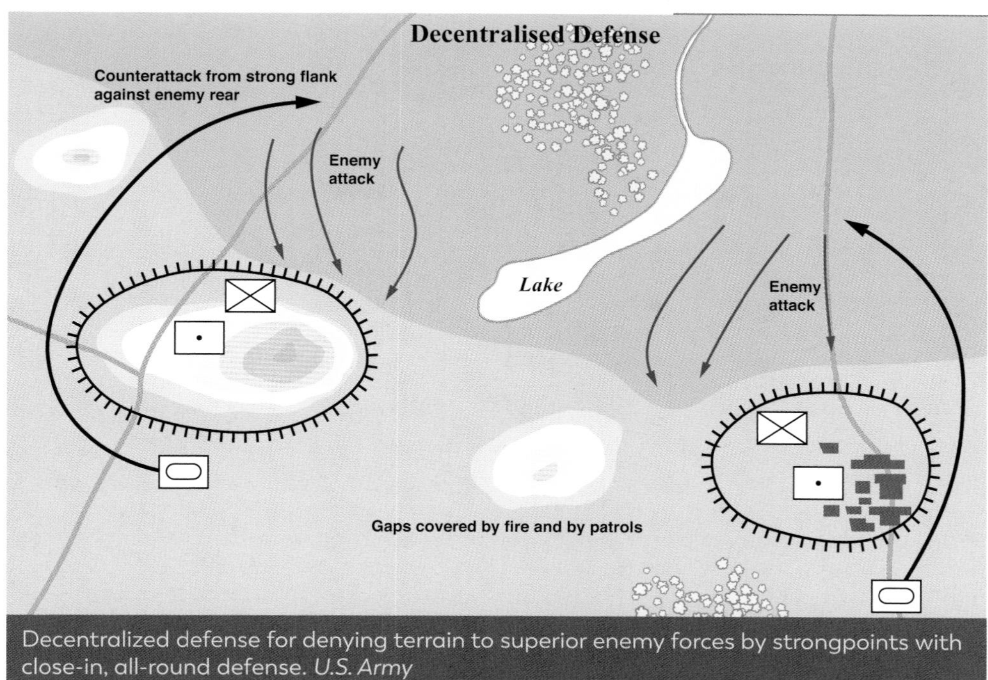

Decentralized defense for denying terrain to superior enemy forces by strongpoints with close-in, all-round defense. *U.S. Army*

a. Centralized defense. This was preferred and was organized to hold the main approaches to important positions with a system of mutually supporting strongpoints. Secondary approaches were covered by fire and by a relatively large mobile reserve. In this type of defense, artillery was massed, counterattacks were initiated by the overall commander, and supply installations were centrally located. Wire communications were established along the main defense axis.

b. Decentralized defense. Undertaken when the forces available for defense of a sector were insufficient for the centralized defense, decentralized defense consisted of a series of self-sufficient islands of defense, each with a local commander, artillery, and supply installations. The reserve of the overall commander was relatively small, and counterattacks were undertaken on the initiative of the local commanders. Communication was accomplished primarily by radio and visual signals.

In general, the defensive positions of an infantry division consisted of an outpost line, a security line, and the main line of resistance (MLR).

- Outpost Line. Designated by an army or divisional commander, it was sited 6–10 miles in front of the MLR. It was intended to inflict losses on the enemy, to disrupt his attack groupments and to gain time. It consisted of forward and intermediate field positions manned by forward detachments.
- Security Line. An infantry division formed a security line 0.5–1 mile in front of the MLR. The purpose of this line was to prevent surprise attacks and to form an anti-reconnaissance screen. It consisted of several strongpoints manned by elements of the forward battalions and supported by their fire. Often, to deceive the enemy, the security line was strengthened in front of dummy positions and weakened in front of the main defensive positions.
- MLR. The main defense line was intended to stop the attack of the hostile infantry and tanks, and to force the enemy to abandon the attack. The MLR was divided into regimental sectors, which were in turn divided into battalion sectors and regimental reserve sectors. Each regimental sector consisted of several centers of resistance which integrated a system of strongpoints for all-around defense. The strongpoints consisted of field and permanent

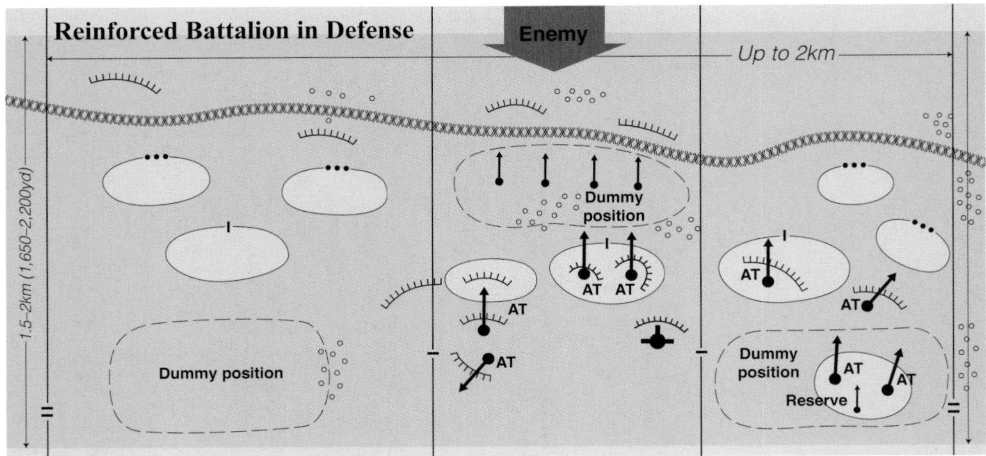

Infantry antitank defenses played a significant role as the Red Army tried to stem German armored attacks. The best-known example is Kursk, where minefields, defenses in depth—antitank ditches and entrenchments prepared with the help of thousands of civilians—and massed artillery blunted the German offensive. *U.S. Army*

fortifications connected by antitank and antipersonnel obstacles, minefields, and traps. The system of obstacles needed to contain gaps for use by counterattacking forces. These gaps were arranged so that they could be quickly closed in the event of enemy penetration of the defenses. The strongpoints were manned either by specially designed garrisons or by elements of the forward battalions. In the former case, the forward battalions occupied positions defending approaches to the strongpoints and supported them with fire. In defending a strong position, the regimental reserve often consisted of a rifle battalion reinforced with artillery, antitank weapons, and tanks. The MLR could only be abandoned on orders of the commander of the next higher echelon.

In organizing defensive positions, the formation of antitank centers of resistance was stressed. These centers, usually located in terrain inaccessible to tanks, consisted of a rifle company with three to five antitank guns, one or two antitank rifle platoons, mortars, and HMGs. Minefields were laid only on orders of the divisional commander. The mission of the infantry was to keep enemy foot soldiers from destroying or neutralizing antitank obstacles. Antiaircraft positions were also chosen in terrain inaccessible to tanks. Careful camouflage and camouflage discipline was emphasized. Defensive combat was controlled from a command post which was not located within the artillery positions. Control of fire, timely commitment of battalion and regimental reserves, and avoidance of premature disclosure of positions and plan of defense were primary considerations in successful defensive combat. During the first stages of enemy attack, artillery fired from alternate positions.

Mine-laying and de-mining played a significant role in defense and attack. *SF collection*

The destruction of tanks and self-propelled guns was an important part of the mission of all artillery, and Red Army crews on all types of artillery were trained in direct fire: antitank defensive barrages were often provided by medium and heavy artillery. The primary tank-destroying weapons were, however, towed antitank guns: the 45mm quickly became outdated but continued to be used alongside the 57mm, 85mm, and 100mm guns—although it was the 76.2mm divisional gun that was the main threat to German tanks. Antitank artillery regiments were often attached to rifle corps and division commanders for the protection of primary sectors, although part of the antitank artillery was kept by the Commander of Combined Arms as a reserve. For example, a quarter of the antitank guns of a rifle division, including regimental and battalion weapons, were held in the mobile divisional antitank gun reserve. Coordination between antitank artillery and other arms, especially field artillery, mortars, engineers, and infantry, was of great importance.

Antitank artillery regiments were also used as tank support in the area of the main effort. Antitank artillery was usually employed in echelons, with weapons of varied caliber in each to ensure equal distribution of firepower. Lighter guns were emplaced as far forward as practicable, although normally not before the second line of infantry trenches. Well dug-in and camouflaged positions, protected by infantry and antitank rifles, were mandatory. Each battery had to have at least one alternate position. When this was occupied, the original position was maintained as a dummy position. Change of position usually took place at night. Antitank guns in each position were placed in a rhombus pattern to obtain all-round fields of fire. Based on experience against enemy armor, the Red Army expected to expend six rounds of fire from 76.2mm antitank guns, or 12 rounds from 45mm antitank guns, for the destruction of one medium tank. They considered that each antitank gun was capable of destroying an average of two to three enemy tanks before it was put out of action.

Antitank fire was directed not only against tanks, but also against accompanying infantry. Such antipersonnel fire was usually supported by mortar units and automatic weapons in coordination with the antitank artillery. Antitank guns continued firing until overrun, since the Red Army considered that the destruction of a large number of enemy tanks represented the successful execution of the mission even when all of its own pieces were lost. As a rule, antitank guns fired at ranges of 550 to 660 yards to avoid revealing prematurely the location of positions. However, when a so-called "firesack" was prepared, a limited number of guns (usually flank pieces) opened fire at the first enemy tank wave at 1,650–2,200-yard ranges and tried to canalize the enemy tanks into the area of the prepared concentration. Reinforcing self-propelled artillery also fired at the tanks from concealed positions.

Urban Warfare

The basic operating unit in city warfare was the rifle battalion, reinforced with armor and antitank groups. When enemy resistance was intense, one city block was designated as the objective for each battalion. The variations in enemy defenses necessitated considerable flexibility in supporting artillery and armor. The battalion was deployed for assault in column formation composed of four distinct groups:

- The infiltration group consisted of a rifle company of two or three platoons and an antitank section. It was armed with automatic weapons, grenades, antitank rifles, and antitank rocket launchers.

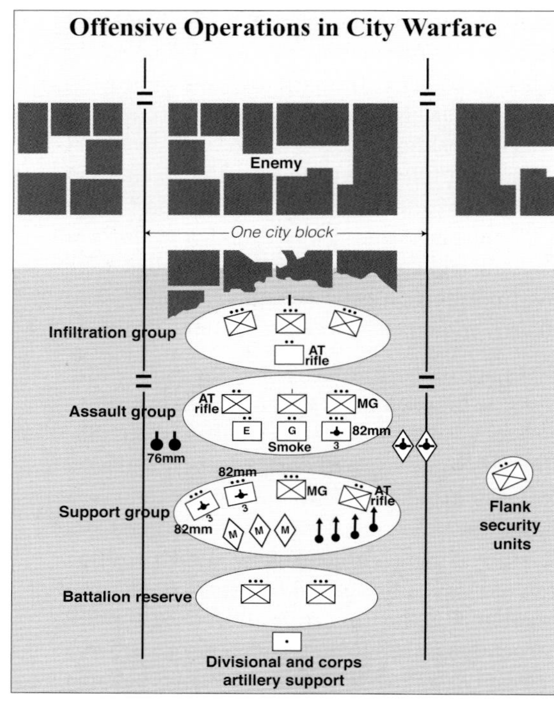

Combat formation of a rifle battalion for offensive operations in an urban environment; close and bloody fighting with no quarter given or taken. Divisional and corps artillery support could be anything up to 10–15 miles to the rear. *U.S. Army*

- The assault group consisted of a rifle company, about half of the battalion heavy weapons, and a detachment of demolition engineers and smoke layers from the rifle regiment. Supporting weapons comprised two to three battalion or regimental direct-fire guns and a platoon of self-propelled guns.
- The support group included the balance of the battalion heavy weapons, three to four regimental or divisional direct-fire guns, and one platoon of medium tanks or self-propelled guns.
- The reserve consisted of one rifle company, which provided flank-security patrols. Subgroups of varying size and composition were detached for separate assault missions on isolated structures. A typical subgroup consisted of seven submachine-gunners, five engineers, three to four heavy machine-gun crews, and two antitank riflemen. Two to four regimental or divisional guns might be placed in support of each subgroup.

Engineers supplemented infantry combat by extensive demining work and by executing demolitions. Tanks used their mobile firepower to supplement artillery. Prior to every assault, coordination plans were developed between the rifle battalion commander and the commanders of artillery and tank support based on their combined reconnaissance. Visual and radio signals were established to indicate when phase lines were reached and for the subordination of supporting artillery and tanks to small subgroups.

Specific techniques were developed by infantry and supporting arms in city warfare. In the assault of a strongly defended city block by a rifle battalion, the support group opened concentrated fire on the windows, doors, and along the flanks of the buildings. Mortar crews fired on intersections and areas to the rear of the block to prevent the enemy from organizing new firing positions. Automatic weapons directed their fire on the upper floors and roofs of buildings, while artillery fire was directed at the lower floors and cellars. Smoke-laying crews threw smoke grenades to cover the approach of tanks and self-propelled guns whose fire was directed toward the center of the block. As soon as a breach was made in the center of the block, the infiltration group dashed through the breach under cover of smoke. Small parties of the infiltration group expanded their operations in all directions, taking positions inside the neutralized buildings to ward off counterattacks. Artillery fire shifted to the enemy position on the flanks. Tanks and self-propelled guns moved into the neutralized sector out of the line of enemy direct fire, concentrating their attention on the corner buildings. The assault group, coordinating its operations with tanks and self-propelled guns, entered the remaining buildings in the block and destroyed the enemy garrison.

An engineer mine-clearing company followed the rifle battalion into newly occupied positions. Each platoon consisted of special mine-clearing subgroups organized as follows: a mine-reconnaissance section of five to six men, a mine-clearing section of eight to ten men, a mine-clearance checking section of four to five men, and a collecting and storing section of two to three men. The engineer company cleared one to two large buildings or 20 to 30 small buildings per day. Demining assignments were planned and controlled by the engineer staff of the formation in charge of the city sector. Tactically important buildings, streets, and blocks were given work-order priority. Trained engineer crews double-checked all important areas, giving special attention to time bombs. In the event that a block was neutralized and seized rapidly, the reserve was committed at once to consolidate the position and to carry the assault to the next block, denying the enemy time to reorganize his system of fire. The support group was displaced forward to engage new enemy firing positions, and the sequence of the operation was repeated. Tanks and self-propelled guns never moved ahead of the infantry, to avoid entering firesacks or detonating landmines. The signals of demining engineers and infantrymen guided the movements of armor.

Sniping

"The Russian sniper has for a long time been a very real factor which has influenced the training of our own infantry," said Hauptmann Borsdorf in the *Hamburger Fremdenblatt*, in May 1944. A German frontline commander said:

> Snipers and mortars inflicted heavy losses on our troops … [In any defensive position] the best places were occupied by the snipers, of which each company had forty to fifty; frequently they were encountered perched on trees and in houses, always well camouflaged and hard to spot.

The Soviet goal was to have three snipers in each platoon, nine in each company or 87 in each regiment. While this may not have been achieved in practice, the Red Army certainly had more snipers and sniper instructors than any other of the belligerents. Many of these were trained by those who had attended the Central Sniper Instructor School, set up on March 20, 1942, in Veshnyaki, Moscow.

Uniquely, the Soviets also trained women in the role of sniper and set up the Central Women's School of Sniper Training, the first class of which graduated in June 1943. Gary Yee:

> Cadets were members of the Young Communist League between 18 and 22 years of age, and candidates were selected on the basis of keen eyesight and prior shooting experience … Classes were taught by lecture and field training. … Sometimes an experienced sniper like Vladimir Pchelintsev visited the school to share his Leningrad sniping experience. … During target practice, they first dug and camouflaged their foxholes before shooting at targets that were full-sized, waist upward, chest upward, running, and fixed.

Lyudmila Pavlichenko, the epitome of the Soviet woman sniper. *Vladimir Nikolayevich IvanovWikiCommons*

Life in the Field

Ilya Shalit: "We were very scared during the first battle. Many people say they were not scared … It's a lie! It was scary: the explosions and the whizz of the bullets all around. I was only thinking about how to stay alive. What is the worst thing about war? It is not the war or the conditions around you. For me personally, the worst thing was to lose my friends and comrades, who became dear to me. We were like brothers. We had our own brotherhood, and it is very difficult to lose your brothers. That was the scariest thing. I remember it to this day. I remember those people … I am already advanced in years—80 years old—but I still remember those who fought next to me but did not survive. That was the scariest thing about the war." (*BA*)

Vasili Tyorkin

The epitome of the Soviet infantryman, Vasili Tyorkin—created by Alexander Tvardovsky—appeared in epic poems published in newspapers and broadcast on the radio. The accordion was an important accompaniment to the bluff everyman as he fought his way to Berlin:

> And out from the iced-over convoy
> There came an eager audience.
> Not caring who was playing or why,
> But yearning for the accordion.

The tunes reminded them of home, "And the accordion calls to them and summons them far away." There are poems about loss—from family to a tobacco pouch; about wounds and death, fighting in swamp and forest, crossing river and plain. Above all, they are about love of country and the lot of the foot soldier:

> Pilots get a lot of love,
> And so do the cavalry.
> But there must be some to give
> To the general infantry!
>
> Yes, the horseman on his horse,
> And yes, the pilot's plane
> But the infantry will face the worst
> Before these other men.

Monument to Tvardovsky and Tyorkin in the city of Smolensk. *Popandopola/ WikiCommons (CC BY-SA 4.0)*

Food

Just about the most important thing for most soldiers is food. By Order 312 of September 20, 1941, of the People's Commissariat, the rations of soldiers and officers were laid out, with a distinction between front and rear troops. This quota was reduced on October 1, 1941, as food-growing areas began to fall into German control.

Foodstuffs	*Front line troops*	*Rear troops*
Bread	800g	600g
Fish	80g	50g
Kasha (grains)	140g	70g
Lard	30g	20g
Meat	150g	75g
Noodles	30g	20g
Oil	20cl	20cl
Salt	30g	30g
Spices	3g	3g
Sugar	35g	20g
Tea	1 gram	1 gram
Tobacco	20g	10g
Vegetables	500g	400g

Non-smoking women received butter, biscuits, and chocolate.

Meals for soldiers were prepared—usually by female cooks—using field kitchens and bakeries that were either hauled along with the unit on a wheeled trailer or placed on the back of a flatbed truck. Each had several cauldrons (between one and four) and a compartment to store food and kitchen utensils.

Because the kitchens burned firewood, the smoke had to be concealed from the enemy by preparing it early—before sunrise—or after dark. Getting hot food to the front line was always difficult.

The main dishes were soups—*kulesh* made from millet, *borshch* (borscht) from beetroot, or *shchi* from cabbage—and buckwheat porridge (*kasha*) or anything available. Hunger wasn't rare. Markus Kleinberg was in a reconnaissance group behind enemy lines:

> We reunited with our side; I won't cover what we experienced while being in the enemy rear. Hunger, especially at the end, because it was winter, we could not go anywhere. We could not light a fire. We built a temporary dugout. We ate whatever we could find. When we were reunited with our forces we were put on a limited diet because after such hunger we could get seriously sick [otherwise]. I cannot say that our command did not want to help us.

An established trench system allows all to eat in relative protection. *SF Collection*

This reproduction smoking set includes in a red calico tobacco pouch: a packet of прибой (The Surf) cigarettes, a packet of бей фашистского гада! (Beat the Nazi bastard!) shag tobacco, and two packs of cigarette papers, which should be enough for a whole pack of shag when used carefully. *Mikhail Moskalev/ Veshchmeshok store*

A field kitchen with a large cauldron smoking away. Smoke was a problem so, ideally, cooking would be done before sunrise or after sunset. *Courtesy of the Central Museum of the Armed Forces, Moscow www.stavka.photos*

> Transport planes flew in several times wanting to drop cargo, but they could not because they were frightened off by antiaircraft guns, so they had to fly away. (*BA*)

Gerts Rogovoy remembers being in the trenches at Kursk in 1943:

> When it all began, we did not see a single one of our planes in the sky, even though it was early 1943. Only the German ones were flying around. They bombed us incessantly. When they released their bombs, I felt as if they were coming right for the top of my head. I just wanted to cover my eyes. Not a single field kitchen would get close enough; we were given no food whatsoever. Some weeks we managed to get a sack of crackers. We chewed on them. We moved at night. During rest breaks we tried to shoot crows and make soup out of them. The best was to find a killed horse. When we found those horses, we would hack pieces off with axes, and tried to cook something. The only things I could not eat were raw potatoes and beets. It was a great joy to be able to boil some potatoes, but the Germans could target you even by the smoke. The hunger was terrible. And I won't lie, we did not bathe. We were infested with lice. (*BA*)

Alexander Gutman remembers 1941:

> Earlier you asked me about food. At first, we had enough to eat. Our kitchen was working, and I kept track of our daily losses in every battalion in order to know how many people needed to be fed. Later we got very little. Every officer had a horse and we had more in reserve. We were supplied with horses. We shot many of them. Our veterinary service would butcher them and serve horsemeat in the kitchen. Later, in October, when we arrived at the Volkhov Front, we received daily rations of 100 grams of crackers and a tin of canned food. That was all. We weren't fed well. (*BA*)

Lev Vengrinovich thought differently:

> In general, we ate well. We got enough. What did a soldier or an officer need? Good *kasha* [buckwheat porridge] or good cabbage soup [there's a famous Russian saying "*shchi da kasha—pishcha nasha*"—cabbage soup and porridge are our food]. 100 grams of combat. What does "100 grams of combat" mean? That was when we were on the offensive. There weren't always combat operations. Sometimes we were in defensive positions. But when there were combat operations, they'd give out an extra 100 grams in the evening with dinner. To lift everyone's mood. It was called "100 Stalin grams." We suffered many losses—we were being killed and bombed—but in the infantry units,

Sending gifts was often linked to holidays: New Year, Red Army Day, or the day of the great October Socialist Revolution. The gifts weren't standardized, comprising whatever the women and children left behind could put together—from stationery and personal hygiene items, to sweets, cigarettes, and matches. This reenactor set comes in a hand-embroidered bag, for a soldier of the Red Army. *Mikhail Moskalev/Veshchmeshok store*

> it would happen that an offensive would start … there would be, say, 150 people in the battalion, and after the battle, 30 would be left alive. The others would be dead or wounded. The warrant officer in charge would have gotten vodka for 150 men. So, they'd drink 300 grams of vodka apiece, not 100. (*BA*)

Arkadiy Dayel remembers the vodka ration:

> There was the so-called front-line ration: we received 50 grams of either vodka or distilled alcohol. I was never addicted, never liked it, and I would give my ration to my friends. Sometimes food was delivered in thermoses. A thermos was about 20 liters; first and second course. Sometimes you'd go off to battle with 20 or 25 people in the company and come back from battle with only 15 men. Some were killed or wounded. But they delivered enough food for the full unit. Sometimes only half the food arrived—the container was damaged during the trip. That's how we ate. When we were in the Baltics, there was lots [of food] in the fields: potatoes, onions, carrots. You could dig some up and get some additional nourishment. (*BA*)

Loot

All armies take trophies and the Red Army was no exception. Initially, when fighting in Soviet territory, these were weapons, consumables (food and drink), and small items—Abram Kotlar:

> We took a lot of spoils of war … [We] stood holding our field caps open in our hands: "Put your watch here! *Gib Messer, Gib Uhr*." I came up to a German, a tall one, and there was a watch on his hand, Wassersport. I said take it off. He didn't want to. I pointed my submachine gun at him so of course he took off his watch and gave it to me. Others didn't want to give their things to us so they dropped their watches to the ground and crushed them, so that our soldiers wouldn't get them. But there were lots of spoils of war. Each of us had at least 10 pairs of watches. Food … we got into their storage and everything that they had … enough to eat and drink. Everything was fine. (*BA*)

Latterly, as the advances entered foreign—and often wealthier—countries, trophies were collected and sent home. From December 1944 this was codified: once a month generals could send home parcels weighing 16kg, officers 10kg, and soldiers 5kg, as long as they had permission from a superior. Extra postal staff had to be put in place to cope with the demand. To send a parcel home it had to be packed in a hard case: Schechter mentions the fact that some units even began to manufacture crates to facilitate this. Some things, however, were banned, particularly written material—even as packing—because of the possibility of corruption of the reader by foreign ideas.

The accordion became a national instrument and the sound of traditional folk music. The photograph shows an interesting range of uniform and weapons. Most wear the winter uniform padded top (*telogreyka*) and padded trousers (*sharovary*), and one appears to be wearing a pair of German camouflage trousers. All wear the *shapka-ushanka* (earflap cap) fur caps, and one carries a bottle, containing alcohol no doubt. The weapons are: on the left, a PPSh-41 with a curved 32-round box magazine and, flanking the accordion player, two PPSh-41s with the 71-round drum magazine. *Fortepan/Vörös Hadsereg*

Triangle letters (**above**) sent from home—from wife Sheva Kantsedikas to her husband, Solomon, on December 21, 1944; and (**below**) to home from the front in October 1943, from I. S. Meerovich to Vera Meerovich in Voronezh. *Blavatnik Archive*

Mail

Sending and receiving letters in wartime was essential for the morale of both the writer, and perhaps more importantly, the recipient in showing that the writer was alive. The classic triangular folding letter was due to the shortage of postcards, paper, and envelopes. It was a letter and envelope in one, needing no stamp. It was forbidden to seal them from the censor who vetted them. A personal observation was the censors were usually lenient and that letters from home were also triangular but needed a stamp. Abram Kotlyar remembered:

> Each unit had a section that took care of the mail. Everyone received mail. I was lucky that I knew where my family evacuated [to]. From Mozdok, my mom and brother, through the Caspian Sea, through Baku; they got to Chkalov Oblast. I found out their address. During the war, the addresses of everyone who was looking for their relatives were collected in the city of Buguruslan. So I knew their address and we wrote each other. (*BA*)

Bathhouse

Arkadiy Dayel:

> I remember a few times we were taken to the rear, to be placed into new formations. In my experience [the rear] was 15 kilometers from the front line. They would bring in a mobile bathhouse in a tent. They'd set up a shower room in there. There was a machine

into which we threw our clothes—our underwear, tunics, pants. That's where they killed the lice. We had lice. There was a time at the front when we sat around the fire and crushed lice.

Newspapers and Magazines

One of the most popular of the forces' newspapers was *Frontline Illustration*, the organ of the Main Political Directorate of the Red Army, which was published 1942–60. It was a wartime photo chronicle using front-line photographers and filmmakers, as well as photomontages. A. Zhitomirskii and B. Shashkov were credited as the main artists. Zhitomirskii also designed *Front Illustrierte für Deutschen Soldaten* with grotesque photomontages against Nazis. It included caricatures by the most notable satirist of the Soviet era—Boris Efimov. Arkadiy Fridner worked on *Defender of the Homeland*, Ninth Army's internal newspaper. They had one freight truck with all their equipment: fonts, plates, printing paper:

> Everything necessary for printing a newspaper, it all fit in this car. ... Overall work went smoothly, typesetters put the papers together and we did not encounter difficulties. ... we published twice a week. Print run wasn't very large, about 3,000 copies. ... We published the newspaper, or tried to, for the ordinary soldier, so that they could understand everything, so that everything would be clear. We didn't get involved much with analyses and discussions. Rather, we focused on specific subjects, specific soldiers and their achievements, specific national news. It was all about what most people were interested in. ... The largest print space, greatest priority, was dedicated to what was happening in our unit, in our division. ... We also published letters. ... These letters provided enormous support for the soldiers, and they awaited their arrival with anticipation. Hence, military post was a very important part of our lives. ... Naturally there was censorship. But honestly, I don't remember meddling or interference. ... Censorship—there was the political division. Personally, they didn't address us. I never noticed major editing of our materials. (*BA*)

Illustrated propaganda postcards were popular methods of communication. This one was printed by the Leningrad Union of Soviet Artists. The newspaper being read is dated to the 24th anniversary of the October Revolution—1941. *Blavatnik Archive*

A typical division—the general combat route of the 13th Guards Rifle Division after its creation on March 4, 1943, from Kharkov to Prague (see numbers in text below).

The Story of the 13th Guards Rifle Division

The journey of the—to give it its full title—13th Guards Rifle "Poltava" bearing the Order of Lenin, twice Order of the Red Banner, Orders of Suvorov and Kutuzov Division during World War II, typifies the failures and successes of the Red Army. It started in early 1936 when the 87th Rifle Division was raised as part of the Kiev Military District in the Korosten Fortified Area. In September 1939, it took part in the annexation of Western Ukraine and the invasion of Poland. On February 12, 1940, the 87th Rifle Division and 128th Motorized Rifle Division (Ural Military District) were mobilized as the XIV Rifle Corps to reinforce the Soviet 8th Army, stationed north of Lake Ladoga, Finland. After the Winter War ended, the corps relocated back to Western Ukraine.

On June 22, 1941, when *Barbarossa* was unleashed, the division was stationed in Ukraine, commanded by Major-General Filipp Fyodorovich Alyabushev. It, 124th, and 135th Rifle Divisions formed the XXVII Rifle Corps, part of the 5th Army of the Southwestern Front. The XXVII Rifle Corps manned the 2nd Fortified Region (Vladimir-Volynsky—VVFR) of the Kiev Special Military District, part of what has become known as the Molotov Line, built 300 kilometers west of the older Stalin Line along the new border with Germany created after the division of Poland. Work had started on the VVFR in 1940 but it wasn't finished: out of 141 planned strongholds, only 97 were operational. Additionally, the division only had two of its rifle regiments in the immediate frontier area. The division was attacked by 6. Armee and Panzergruppe 1 of Heeresgruppe Süd and was involved in heavy fighting during the battle of Lutsk-Rovno. By June 24 the division was encircled and attempts by the 16th Rifle Regiment to break through to the surrounded units failed. On the 25th Alyabushev died leading a bayonet charge attempting to break through surrounding German forces. Finally, on July 1 200 men under the command of Colonel M. I. Blanka, together with the division's banners, broke out of the encirclement and withdrew east, eventually being withdrawn from action for reinforcement and recovery.

87th Rifle Division in 1941

16th, 96th and 283rd Rifle Regts
197th Artillery Regt
212th Howitzer Artillery Regt
85th Separate Anti-Tank Artillery Bn
14th Separate Anti-Aircraft Artillery Bn
43rd Reconnaissance Bn
11th Sapper Bn
14th Separate Communications Bn
59th Medical-Sanitary Bn
119th Separate Chemical Defence Co
86th Auto Transport Co
137th Field Bakery
403rd Field Cash Office

In August 1941 the rebuilt division was transferred to 37th Army and took part in the defense of Kiev under the command of Colonel Nikolay Ivanovich Vasilyev, who had been Deputy Divisional Commander since May 1940. The battle for Kiev took place between August 23 and September 26, 1941, during which the division was surrounded and destroyed. Colonel Vasilyev was killed.

On November 6, 1941, the 87th Rifle Division was reformed under the command of Colonel Alexander Rodimtsev from its surviving members, III Airborne Corps, and staff from 5th Airborne Brigade, and on November 20, 1941, became an active field unit with the 40th Army in the Kursk District. The 87th's order of battle was as before but without the 212th Howitzer Artillery Regiment.

The Germans continued to push the Russian forces east and on December 4 broke through 40th Army's defensive front. The division was tasked to close the breach. There was intense fighting in December 1941 and January 1942, during which the Germans were pushed back and on January 19 the 87th Division was honored by conversion into a Guards division for its actions during these battles. It was officially awarded the title of the 13th Guards Rifle Division and received its banner on March 4, 1942. Rodimtsev commanded the new division as part of the 28th Army of the Southwestern Front.

On March 27, 1942, the 13th Guards received the Order of Lenin for the courage, bravery, and success of its winter operations. As part of the 28th Army, in May 1942 the division took part in the second battle of Kharkov (**1** on map). Initial advances were halted by German counterattacks and heavy fighting ensued during which the division was forced east to avoid encirclement. Losses were heavy—around half its strength—and once again the division was withdrawn from the front line to be rebuilt. While it received reinforcements, the division became part of the Army Reserve positioned on the Volga 180 kilometers north of Stalingrad. During the Kharkov campaign, on May 21, 1942, Colonel Rodimtsev was promoted to major-general.

A few weeks later, in July, the German campaign to take Stalingrad began. They advanced swiftly, pushing the Soviet forces back into the city which was then bombed heavily by the Luftwaffe. By the end of August, 6. Armee had closed off the city and was threatening the main ferry crossing. Late on September 11, the 13th Guards was ordered to Stalingrad (**2**). It marched immediately, the lead elements covering the 180 kilometers in 48 hours. At this stage the division consisted of just under 10,000 men, mainly inexperienced troops. They were not only underequipped and low on ammunition but 1,000 rifles short of the established TO&E—mainly in the divisional rear services and artillery units on the east bank of the river and rather than front-line rifle battalions about to

13th Guards Division in 1942

34th, 39th and 42nd Guards Rifle Regts (formerly 16th, 96th and 283rd Regts)
32nd Guards Artillery Regt
4th Guards Anti-Tank Bn
8th Guards Sapper Bn
14th Reconnaissance Co
39th Signal Bn
12th Chemical Warfare Co
11th Transport Co
17th Field Bakery
15th Medical Bn
2nd Veterinary Hospital

go into battle in the city. Additionally, once the issue was raised, weapons—including SMGs which were best for urban conditions—were collected and provided by other units.

So, late on September 14, the 1st Battalion, 42nd Guards Rifle Regiment used whatever means at its disposal to cross the Volga and secure a bridgehead for the rest of the division. Severe casualties were sustained but the rest of the regiment followed and joined elements of 10th NKVD Division. They managed to push the Germans back, helped by the Guards' second wave—the 39th Guards Rifle Regiment. The division's intervention was as costly as it was crucial: fully 30 percent were killed in the first 24 hours of landing and within a week that figure had more than doubled. But it held the Germans and Marshal Vasily Chuikov, commander of Soviet 62nd Army, later said: "Frankly, if it were not for Rodimtsev's division, the city would have been completely in the hands of the enemy back in September."

Rodimtsev, a veteran of the Spanish Civil War and a veteran of urban fighting, used all his experience and considerable bravery during the fighting at Mamayev Kurgan and the railway station and his prowess was rewarded when he was promoted to command XXXII Guards Rifle Corps. The 13th Guards was part of this corps under a new divisional commander, Major-General Gleb Vladimirovich Baklanov.

Next up for this much-decorated unit was the battle of Kursk (**3**). After refit and resupply between February 5 and April 6, on the 16th of that month it arrived at Talovaya, southeast of Voronezh, and became part of the Steppe Military District Army Reserve under 5th Guards Army. Kursk is remembered for the German armored assault on Soviet prepared lines of defense—and while there were huge tank battles, much of the fighting was by the infantry, antitank, and artillery units, whose killing zones negated German tactical advantages.

The German attack was powerful enough to force the Stavka to use its reserves and the 5th Guards Army was committed on July 6. The battle hung in the balance, with German airpower an important factor, but the invaders had underestimated the size of the Soviet reserves and Hitler was forced to order withdrawal on July 17. Both sides retired to lick their wounds—but the Soviet response was faster than the Germans expected and more deadly: on August 3 Operation *Polkovodets Rumyantsev* saw the 5th Guards Army regain Belgorod (**4**) and Kharkov (**5**).

On September 7, 1943, the 5th Guards Army left the Voronezh Front and became part of the Steppe Front. The race to the Dnieper began, held up by tough fighting around Poltava (**6**), which was liberated on September 23, for which the participating units—including 13th Guards—were awarded the honorary title "Poltava."

On September 15, 1943, Hitler allowed the German forces to move back to prepared positions—the Panther (in the north) and Wotan lines, referred to as the Ostwall—along the Dnieper and other rivers. The Dnieper itself was a mighty obstacle, in places over two miles wide, and provided a significant defensive barrier. The lines had been built quickly—the construction order was signed on August 11, 1943—by a mixture of Organization Todt, Ost-Baupionier-Bataillone, POWs, and local labor, and consisted of bunkers, trenches, MG positions, barbed wire, minefields, etc. Many of the positions were incomplete. However, the Soviets didn't allow the Germans time to sort out these problems. They made their way across the river in as many places as possible—particularly in the weakest area of the defenses, the south—holding onto the bridgeheads against sustained counterattacks and even attempted airborne operations although these had disastrous results with heavy casualties.

The 13th Guards took part in a feint crossing operation near Kremenchug on the night of October 5. By the time the division withdrew, Soviet forces had been able to force crossings and establish bridgeheads both upstream and downstream of Kremenchug (**7**). When the dust settled the Soviets had a 300-kilometer-wide bridgehead, in places up to 80 kilometers deep. Added to this, by overrunning the southern end of the defenses, they had cut off the Crimea and the German 17. Armee.

The end of 1943 and early 1944 saw the Soviet forces take back even more territory, relieving the siege of Leningrad in the north and in the south liberating the rest of Ukraine. The 13th Guards—as part of 5th Guards Army under the Second Ukrainian Front (General Ivan Konev's renamed Steppe Front)—took part in the Kirovograd (**8** January–February 1944) and Uman-Botosani (March 5–April 17) offensive operations, advancing over 300 kilometers over six major rivers, reaching the Romanian border and inflicting heavy losses on the Germans. During the battles the 13th Guards added to its honors, first with the liberation of the city of Novoukrainka (**9**) for which it received a second Order of the Red Banner, and then at Pervomaysk (**10**) and the crossing of the River Southern Bug, when it was awarded the Order of Suvorov II class. It ended fighting in the Serpeni Bridgeheadnear Kishinev, capital of Moldova (**11**).

The 13th Guards went into Stavka reserve south of Ternopol (**12**) with the 5th Guards Army on June 26. On July 13 the army was transferred to the First Ukrainian Front. During July and August, the division fought in the Lvov–Sandomierz (**13**) offensive. Colonel Gleb Balkanov, the divisional commander, was promoted after the offensive and took over XXXIV Guards Rifle Corps. Command of 13th Guards went to Colonel Vladimir N. Komarov.

1945 saw the 13th Guards fighting in the Vistula–Oder offensive, liberating the Polish towns of Busko-Zdrój on January 13 and Częstochowa (**14**) on the 17th. On the 19th the division crossed the German border and spent February and early March fighting in Silesia (**15**) before playing its part in the administration of the last rites to the Third Reich. 13th Guards forced the Neisse and Spree rivers before reaching Torgau (**16**) on the River Elbe on April 23. There it met elements of the First (U.S.) Army. The battle on the Neisse saw the division awarded the Order of Kutuzov II Class on May 28.

The division's final offensive was significant for the political map of postwar Europe, as the Soviet forces rapidly punched south and from the east to take Prague. At a time when remaining German resistance in the area was seriously crumbling, the division en route took part in capturing Dresden (**17**) on May 8 and having crossed the Ore Mountains into Czechoslovakia, was present when Theresienstadt concentration camp at was liberated on May 9. Finally, it took part in clearing up final resistance in the Kladno area, northwest of Prague (**18**), on May 11/12, three days after the declaration of VE-Day.

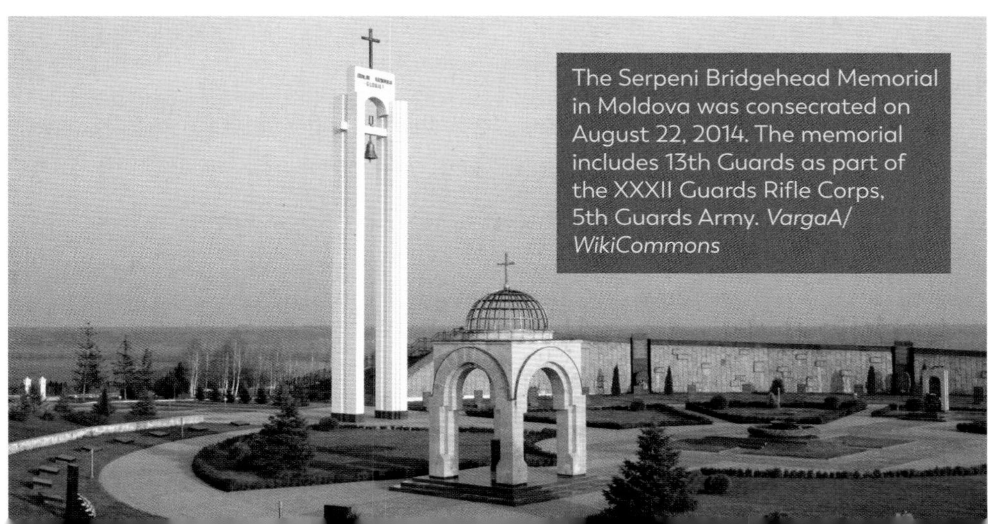

The Serpeni Bridgehead Memorial in Moldova was consecrated on August 22, 2014. The memorial includes 13th Guards as part of the XXXII Guards Rifle Corps, 5th Guards Army. *VargaA/ WikiCommons*

Conclusion

The Western view of the Soviet infantryman and Red Army is colored by the Cold War. As the Soviet Union moved from valued ally to likely adversary, the Eastern Front battles were dissected by the German generals who had fought them. They pushed their own agendas and tended to undervalue their opponents, blaming the German defeat on Soviet hordes, poor strategy from the top, and almost anything other than the prowess of the Red Army.

In fact, the story of the Eastern Front was very similar to that of the west, albeit on a greater scale. Initial crushing victories were not enough to knock the Soviets out. The Red Army learned how to fight a modern war, as did the Western allies. It took them time, and that time was won by the sacrifice of millions of Soviet soldiers, many of them infantry. These men—and women, for the Red Army employed many—were not simply cannon fodder. They were committed, patriotic young people who fought for their country and their cause. Politicized by communism, they believed their leaders' rhetoric and—scared, sometimes fatalistic, but often with great courage—they finally stopped the Germans before they could deliver the final knockout blow.

The Red Army grew in stature after its winter 1941–42 counterattack successes and the later victories at Stalingrad and Kursk, just as the Western allies did after victory in North Africa. The Red Army's plentiful artillery, workmanlike weaponry, and the remarkable durability and tenacity of their infantry ground down its opponents. Once the floodgates opened, the Soviet forces rapidly advanced and showed amongst other things that their logistics support and transport—the latter significantly helped by Lend-Lease—were much better than their enemy's.

At the last, the Soviet soldiers took their revenge on the German people and their allies as they pushed over their borders. They had been taught to hate, but many of them didn't need to be. They had seen for themselves what the invaders had done: the massacres, the extermination camps, and the maltreatment of POWs. Those who endured the backlash often used the excesses of the Red Army as camouflage for their involvement in the Nazi regime. The rapes and pillaging perpetrated by the Soviets can never be condoned, but it can be understood.

Further Reading

Baxter, Ian: *Kursk 1943: Last German Offensive in the East*; Casemate Publishers, 2020.

Baxter, Ian: *The Soviet Baltic Offensive, 1944–45: German Defense of Estonia, Latvia, and Lithuania*; Casemate Publishers, 2022.

Baxter, Ian: *Operation* Bagration*: The Soviet Destruction of German Army Group Center, 1944*; Casemate Publishers, 2020.

Baxter, Ian: *The Soviet Destruction of Army Group South: Ukraine and Southern Poland 1943–1945*; Casemate Publishers, 2023.

Buffetaut, Yves: *From Moscow to Stalingrad: The Eastern Front, 1941–1942*: Casemate Publishers, 2018.

Bullock, Alan: *Hitler and Stalin: Parallel Lives*; Vintage Books, 1993.

Davie, H. G. W.: "The Influence of Railways on Military Operations in the Russo-German War 1941–1945," *The Journal of Slavic Military Studies*, April 2017. DOI: *10.1080/13518046.2017.1308120*.

Davie, H. G. W.: "The reality of modernity—Motor vehicles in the Red Army"; 2018. www.hgwdavie.com/blog/2017/6/22/the-reality-of-modernity.

De Jesus Reyes, Michelle: "Experiences of Soviet Women Combatants During World War II"; History theses, 2017 via http://digitalcommons.buffalostate.edu/history_theses/41

Dept of the Army pamphlets *20-230 Russian Combat Methods in World War II*; *20-290 Terrain Factors in the Russian Campaign*; Washington, D.C., 1950–51; *C-058 Experience Gained in Combat Against Soviet Infantry*; USAREUR, 1950.

Grossman, Vasily (Ed./Translators Anthony Beevor & Luba Vinogradova): *A Writer at War*; Pimlico, 2006.

Glantz, David M.: *The Soviet-German War 1941–1945: Myths and Realities: A Survey Essay*; Clemson University, SC, 2001.

Glantz, David M. & House, Jonathan M.: *When Titans Clashed: How the Red Army Stopped Hitler*; University Press of Kansas, 2015.

Grant, Susan: *Soviet Nightingales—Care Under Communism*; Cornell University, 2022 via https://d119vjm4apzmdm.cloudfront.net/open-access/pdfs/9781501762604.pdf.

Halder, Franz & Lissance, Arnold (Ed.): *War Journal of Franz Halder* vols VI and VII; AG EUCOM.

Liedtke, Gregory: *Wolverhampton Military Studies No. 21, Enduring the Whirlwind*; Helion & Company, 2016.

Merridale, Catherine: *Ivan's War: The Red Army 1939–45*; Faber & Faber Ltd, 2005.

Naud, Philippe: *Operation* Typhoon*: The German Assault on Moscow, 1941*; Casemate Publishers, 2018.

Pennell, Catriona & de Meneses, Filipe Ribeiro: *A World At War, 1911–1949: Explorations in the Cultural History of War: 124 (History of Warfare)*; Brill, 2019.

Pennington, Reina: "Offensive Women: Women in Combat in the Red Army in the Second World War"; *The Journal of Military History* 74 (July 2010), pp. 775–820.

Reese, Roger: *Why Stalin's Soldiers Fought: The Red Army's Military Effectiveness in World War II*; University Press of Kansas, 2011.

Rottman, Gordon L. & Gerrard, Howard: *Warrior 123 Soviet Rifleman 1941–45*; Osprey Publishing, 2007.

Rottman, Gordon L., Taylor, Chris & Delf, Brian: *Fortress 62 Soviet Field Fortifications 1941–45*; Osprey Publishing, 2007.

Sánchez Cózar, Irene: "The Invisible Combatants of World War II: Soviet Female Soldiers in the Socialist State"; Global Strategy Report, No 11/2022.

Schechter, Brandon M.: "'Girls' and 'Women.' Love, Sex, Duty and Sexual Harassment in the Ranks of the Red Army 1941–1945;" *Journal of Power Institutions in Post-Soviet Societies*, Issue 17, 2016 (https://doi.org/10.4000/pipss.4202).

Schechter, Brandon M.: *The Stuff of Soldiers: A History of the Red Army in World War II Through Objects*; Cornell University Press, 2019.

Short, Neil & Hook, Adam: *Fortress 77 The Stalin and Molotov Lines*; Osprey Publishing, 2008.

Slepyan, Kenneth: "Why They Fought: Motivation, Legitimacy and the Soviet Partisan Movement"; NCEEER, 2003.

Thomas, Nigel & Abbott, Peter: *Men at Arms 142 Partisan Warfare 1941–45*; Osprey Publishing, 1983.

Thomas, Nigel & Pavlovic, Darko: *Men at Arms 464, 468, 469 World War II Soviet Armed Forces (1. 1939–41; 2. 1942–43; 3 1944–45)*; Osprey Publishing, 2010–12.

Transcript of Proceedings, Art of War Symposia: *1. From the Don to the Dnepr: Soviet offensive operations—December 1942–August 1943*; *2. From the Dnepr to the Vistula: Soviet offensive operations—November 1943–August 1944*; *3. From the Vistula to the Oder: Soviet offensive operations—October 1944–March 1945*; Center for Land Warfare, U.S. Army War College, 1984–86.

War Department (U.S.) & Bolin, Robert L., Depositor: *Handbook on USSR Military Forces*, Chapters III "Field Organization, V Tactics," VI "Fortifications," VII "Logistics," IX "Equipment;" DOD Military Intelligence, 1946 via http://digitalcommons.unl.edu/dodmilintel.

Yee, Gary: *World War II Snipers: The Men, Their Guns, Their Stories*; Casemate Publishers, 2023.

Zaloga, Stephen J. & Volstad, Ron: *Men at Arms 216 The Red Army of the Great Patriotic War 1941–45*; Osprey Publishing, 1984.

Index